Altered State?

Assessing How Marijuana Legalization in California Could Influence Marijuana Consumption and Public Budgets

Beau Kilmer, Jonathan P. Caulkins,

Rosalie Liccardo Pacula, Robert J. MacCoun,

Peter H. Reuter

Drug Policy Research Center

A JOINT ENDEAVOR OF RAND HEALTH AND
RAND INFRASTRUCTURE, SAFETY, AND ENVIRONMENT

Funding for this paper was provided by RAND's Investment in People and Ideas program, which combines philanthropic contributions from individuals, foundations, and private-sector firms with earnings from RAND's endowment and operations to support research on issues that reach beyond the scope of traditional client sponsorship. This research was conducted under the auspices of the RAND Drug Policy Research Center, a joint endeavor of RAND Health and RAND Infrastructure, Safety, and Environment.

Library of Congress Control Number: 2010931677

ISBN 978-0-8330-5034-2

Published 2010 by the RAND Corporation
1776 Main Street, P.O. Box 2138, Santa Monica, CA 90407-2138
1200 South Hayes Street, Arlington, VA 22202-5050
4570 Fifth Avenue, Suite 600, Pittsburgh, PA 15213-2665
RAND URL: http://www.rand.org/
To order RAND documents or to obtain additional information, contact
Distribution Services: Telephone: (310) 451-7002;
Fax: (310) 451-6915; Email: order@rand.org

Preface

California Assembly Bill 2254—often referred to as the Ammiano bill—and the Regulate, Control, and Tax Cannabis (RCTC) proposition would legalize marijuana use for those 21 and over in California. The Ammiano bill would allow the state to regulate production and distribution and initially apply an excise tax of $50 per ounce. The RCTC proposition would allow local governments to choose whether and how to regulate and tax production and distribution.

Two issues central to the debate are how legalization would affect marijuana consumption and public budgets. Governor Arnold Schwarzenegger suggested that "it was time for a debate" about legalization to generate revenue, and one government analysis estimated that taxing marijuana at $50 per ounce would generate $1.4 billion annually in revenues.

In this occasional paper, researchers addressed these two issues by constructing a model based on a series of estimates of current consumption, current and future prices, how responsive use is to price changes, taxes levied and possibly evaded, and the aggregation of nonprice effects (such as changes in attitudes).

This occasional paper results from the RAND Corporation's Investment in People and Ideas program. Support for this program is provided, in part, by the generosity of RAND's donors and by the fees earned on client-funded research.

Rosalie Liccardo Pacula is a recipient of a 2010 RAND President's Award. One vehicle through which RAND invests in people, President's Awards recognize individuals who have made outstanding contributions to the RAND community while exemplifying RAND's core values of quality and objectivity. Made possible by the generosity of donors to the RAND Policy Circle, the awards provide staff with research time and support to pursue activities related to career development or exploratory research.

This project did not have an external sponsor; the time used to conduct the work was either donated by the authors or internally funded by two of the RAND Corporation's units: RAND Health and RAND Infrastructure, Safety, and Environment.

The RAND Drug Policy Research Center

This study was conducted under the auspices of the RAND Drug Policy Research Center, a joint endeavor of RAND Health and RAND Infrastructure, Safety, and Environment. The goal of the Drug Policy Research Center is to provide a firm, empirical foundation on which sound drug policies can be built, at the local and national levels. The center's work is supported by foundations, government agencies, corporations, and individuals.

Questions or comments about this paper should be sent to the project leader, Beau Kilmer (Beau_Kilmer@rand.org). Information about the Drug Policy Research Center is available online (http://www.rand.org/multi/dprc/). Inquiries about research projects should be made to the center's co-directors, Rosalie Liccardo Pacula (Rosalie_Pacula@rand.org) and Beau Kilmer (Beau_Kilmer@rand.org).

Contents

Figures

Tables

Acknowledgments

We are deeply indebted to the Carnegie Mellon Heinz students who provided background research and analysis for this paper, particularly Brittany Bond, Leigh Halverson, Dawn Holmes, Ben Horwitz, Lynly Lumibao, Eric Morris, and Rhajiv Ratnatunga. We are especially grateful to Wayne Hall and Mireille Jacobson for their excellent reviews. We also thank Monica Banken, Martin Bouchard, Dale Gieringer, Erin Kilmer Neel, Mark Kleiman, Sarah Lawrence, Nancy Nicosia, and Greg Ridgeway for their insights. As always, Jim Burgdorf provided excellent research assistance. This work represents the views of only the authors.

Abbreviations

AB	Assembly bill
ABC	Department of Alcoholic Beverage Control
ADAM	Arrestee Drug Abuse Monitoring Program
ADP	Department of Alcohol and Drug Programs
BOE	California State Board of Equalization
DSM-IV	*Diagnostic and Statistical Manual of Mental Disorders*, 4th ed.
ED	emergency department
FARS	Fatality Analysis Reporting System
FY	fiscal year
HHS	U.S. Department of Health and Human Services
LAO	Legislative Analyst's Office
LAPD	Los Angeles Police Department
MT	metric ton
NHSDA	National Household Survey on Drug Abuse
NORML	National Organization for the Reform of Marijuana Laws
NSDUH	National Survey on Drug Use and Health
OSHPD	Office of Statewide Health Planning and Development
RCTC	Regulate, Control, and Tax Cannabis
SB	Senate bill
TEDS	Treatment Episode Data Set
THC	delta-9-tetrahydrocannabinol
UNODC	United Nations Office on Drugs and Crime

CHAPTER ONE

Introduction

California has always been on the cutting edge of marijuana policy reform. It was one of the first states to prohibit marijuana in 1913, predating the federal Marihuana Tax Act of 1937 (Pub. L. 75-238)[1] by nearly 25 years (Gieringer, 2006). In 1975, California was one of the first states to reduce the maximum sentence for possessing less than an ounce from incarceration to a small fine ($100). In 1996, California was the first state to allow marijuana to be grown and consumed for medicinal purposes. And, in November 2010, California will become the third state to vote on whether marijuana should be legalized and taxed—and potentially the first to pass such legislation.[2]

While Californians have discussed legalization for decades, the idea is now being taken more seriously by policymakers, pundits, and the population at large. It was noteworthy when Republican Governor Arnold Schwarzenegger suggested that "it was time for a debate" about marijuana legalization as a way of increasing state revenues. There has been a flurry of activity in Sacramento, including an October 2009 hearing of the California Assembly Committee on Public Safety and the introduction of two marijuana reform bills in 2010. The debate has gained considerable attention because of the recession and California's budget crisis, and it has been fueled by a report from the California State Board of Equalization (BOE) estimating that legalizing marijuana and taxing it at $50 per ounce would generate $1.4 billion for the state each year.

Within this context, this RAND occasional paper is intended to inform the debate about marijuana legalization in California. Although marijuana legalization could have many consequences, this paper focuses largely on two outcomes that are central to the debate in California: the effect on consumption and public budgets.

To learn more about the possible outcomes of marijuana legalization, we constructed a model based on a series of estimates. As we discuss in more detail in Chapter Three, projections of legalization's effects on consumption and public budgets hinge on estimates of current consumption, current and future prices, how responsive use is to price changes (what economists refer to as the *price elasticity of demand*), taxes levied and possibly evaded, and the aggregation of many nonprice effects (such as the potential reduction in stigma). These components, or parameters, of the model are then combined to produce a base-case model estimate. Our

---

[1] The Marihuana Tax Act was modeled after the Harrison Act, which imposed major restrictions on opiates and cocaine (Bonnie and Whitebread, 1970). Musto (1972) reports that, aside from the Federal Food and Drugs Act of 1906 (Pub. L. 59-384), the Marihuana Tax Act of 1937 was the first federal law that was targeted at marijuana. He notes that, "By 1931 regulations under the Food and Drug Act [sic] had limited the importation of cannabis except for medical purposes."

[2] Nevada voters rejected a related proposition in 2006, and Alaska voters rejected two ballot propositions (2000, 2004) that would have allowed the state to regulate marijuana sales.

intent is to systematically think through the factors that influence the two outcomes and help decisionmakers understand the impact of key uncertainties that surround those factors. We stress that the current analysis is not intended to provide a comprehensive cost-benefit analysis of the impact of legalizing marijuana in California.

Our analysis reveals that projections about the impact of legalizing marijuana in California on consumption and public budgets are subject to considerable uncertainty. Although the state could see large increases in consumption and substantial positive budget effects, it could also see increases in consumption and low revenues due to tax evasion or a "race to the bottom" in terms of local tax rates.

Decisionmakers should view skeptically any projections that claim either precision or accuracy. In particular, we highlight two distinct drivers of uncertainty that surround these estimates of consumption and tax revenues: uncertainty about parameters (such as how legalization will affect production costs and price) and uncertainty about structural assumptions (such as the federal response to a state that allows production and distribution of a substance that would still be illegal under federal law). Such uncertainties are so large that altering just a few key assumptions or parameter values can dramatically change the results.[3]

With that crucial caveat in mind, we offer the following key insights derived from developing and using this model:

- The pretax retail price of marijuana will substantially decline, likely by more than 80 percent. The price that consumers face will depend heavily on taxes, the structure of the regulatory regime, and how taxes and regulations are enforced.
- Consumption will increase, but it is unclear how much because we know neither the shape of the demand curve nor the level of tax evasion (which reduces revenues and the prices that consumers face).
- Tax revenues could be dramatically lower or higher than the $1.4 billion estimate; for example, there is uncertainty about potential tax revenues that California might derive from taxing marijuana used by residents of other states (e.g., from "drug tourism").
- Previous studies find that the annual costs of enforcing marijuana laws range from around $200 million to nearly $1.9 billion; our estimates show that the costs are probably less than $300 million.
- There is considerable uncertainty about the impact of legalizing marijuana in California on public budgets and consumption, with even minor changes in assumptions leading to major differences in outcomes.
- Much of the research used to inform this debate is based on insights from studies that examine small changes in either marijuana prices or the risk of being sanctioned for possession. The proposed legislation in California would create a large change in policy. As a result, it is uncertain how useful these studies are for making projections about marijuana legalization.

The paper is organized as follows. Chapter Two provides some context about current marijuana use and policy in California, including a review of the proposition and the two

---

[3] Many of the results presented in this occasional paper are drawn from nine more-detailed documents: Bond and Caulkins (2010); Caulkins (2010a, 2010b); Caulkins, Morris, and Ratnatunga (2010); MacCoun (2010b, 2010c); Pacula (2010a, 2010b); and Reuter (2010).

marijuana policy reform bills being considered by the California legislature in June 2010. It also briefly describes the variety of marijuana policies in other countries. Chapter Three discusses the factors needed to make projections about the effect of legalization, showing how we combine those factors into a model related to the effects we are studying and concluding with our thoughts about best values for some key parameters. Chapter Four demonstrates the uncertainty surrounding the results of the base-case scenario when plausible alternative inputs are used for just a few key factors, and Chapter Five discusses other important outcomes, such as criminal-justice savings, treatment costs, and nonbudgetary effects. Chapter Six considers alternative scenarios, and Chapter Seven offers some concluding thoughts.

CHAPTER TWO

The Marijuana Landscape in California

This chapter provides information about current marijuana use and policies in California. It covers many topics lightly; some are covered in more detail later, when the components of the legalization regime effects are being considered.

Consumption

Rates of marijuana use in California are fairly similar to those of the rest of the country.[1] The percentage of Californians age 12 or over reporting use of marijuana in the previous 30 days was 7 percent circa 2007, compared to 6 percent for the rest of the nation. For the youngest category, those ages 12–17, the difference between California and the rest of the nation is even smaller. There are also strong similarities in the rates for alcohol and cocaine use, but not for past-month tobacco use, for which the rate is 29 percent for the nation and only 23 percent for California.

Table 2.1 shows changes between 2002 and 2007 in the number of past-month and past-year users in California, both for those 12 and over and for those 12–17.[2] None of the series gives any indication of increasing prevalence in recent years, which is consistent with the long-term pattern for the United States: Since about 1990, prevalence for the population 12 and over has been very stable, even as rates for adolescents and young adults have fluctuated substantially. That variability in the rate for younger users is also reflected in the California data.

There is substantial variation in usage rates across regions of the state, with the highest rate in Northern California, which is also the center of the state's marijuana production (Figure 2.1). The lowest rates are in Los Angeles County, Santa Clara County, and the central interior regions of the state.

---

[1] These data come from the National Survey on Drug Use and Health (NSDUH), a large (n = 65,000+) annual survey conducted by the U.S. Department of Health and Human Services (HHS). Although the survey is known to underestimate the number of frequent users of such drugs as cocaine and heroin (Wright, Gfroerer, and Epstein, 1997), it is thought to provide acceptable estimates for marijuana, albeit with some underreporting. After reviewing studies of underreporting specifically for marijuana, Kilmer and Pacula (2009) suggest that perhaps 20 percent of respondents failed to report that they had used marijuana.

[2] The series starts with the year 2002 because improvements in survey methodology that year led to a higher level of reporting of drug use; it is not possible to compare 2002 and later with earlier years. State-level estimates are published only with the concatenation of two years of data; 2006–2007 is the most recent year-pair for which estimates have been published.

Table 2.1
Marijuana Use in California, 2002–2007

| | Past 30 Days | | | | Annual | | | |
| | 12+ Years Old | | 12–17 Years Old | | 12+ Years Old | | 12–17 Years Old | |
Year	Number (000s)	Rate (%)	Number (000s)	Rate (%)	Number (000s)	Rate (%)	Number (000s)	Rate (%)
2002–2003	1,850	6.4	241	7.7	3,222	11.2	443	14.1
2003–2004	1,933	6.6	273	8.6	3,192	11.0	469	14.8
2004–2005	1,951	6.6	247	7.8	3,322	11.3	458	14.4
2005–2006	1,970	6.6	215	6.8	3,336	11.3	433	13.6
2006–2007	1,949	6.5	222	7.0	3,342	11.2	424	13.4

SOURCE: SAMHSA (annual).

Figure 2.1
Geographic Variation in Past-Month Marijuana Use in California, 2004–2006

SOURCES: SAMHSA (2005, 2006, 2007).
NOTE: Based on those aged 12 and older.
RAND OP315-2.1

Treatment

A recent phenomenon in both the United States and other Western countries is a substantial increase in the number of individuals seeking treatment for marijuana abuse or dependence. Nationally, marijuana now accounts for the largest number of treatment episodes (excluding alcohol)—about 322,000 in 2008, compared to 92,500 in 1992.[3] In that period, the share of treatment admissions for which marijuana was the primary drug grew from about 6 percent to 17 percent (HHS, 2009). California has seen an even larger increase, with a near quintupling of the number of marijuana admissions between 1992 and 2008 (7,300 and almost 35,000, respectively), while the total number of treatment admissions for illicit drugs increased 50 percent during that period.

One interpretation of the rise in treatment admissions is that it reflects increasing enforcement of marijuana laws; in that sense, people seek treatment less to deal with a substance-abuse problem than to manage a legal problem. However, other countries, including the Netherlands, where users are not subject to criminal-justice pressure, have seen a similar increase, which indicates that there might be other factors driving this phenomenon (EMCDDA, 2009; MacCoun, 2010c).

Arrests and Dispositions

Marijuana offenses account for most of the drug arrests in the United States, and the number has risen sharply in the past 20 years. More than 80 percent of marijuana arrests are now for simple possession. The rate of possession arrests per capita rose sharply in the United States in the 1990s, from about 89 per 100,000 population in 1991 to 223 in 1997 (Figure 2.2). Since then, the number has risen more slowly, approaching 250 per 100,000 in 2008 (about 750,000 arrests in total). Sales arrests rose much more slowly from 1990 to 2008; instead of the nearly 200-percent increase for possession, sales arrests nationally rose only about 40 percent between 1990 and 2008.

While per capita marijuana arrests were similar for the United States and California in the early 1990s, the subsequent increase was more pronounced outside of California. Still, the arrest data for California also show a dramatic increase from 1990 to 1996. Per capita marijuana arrests in California remained stable between 1996 and 2005 (around 175 per 100,000) and then jumped more than 25 percent between 2005 and 2008. Although not pictured here, there was a large increase in total juvenile marijuana arrests in California in the early 1990s, but that number soon stabilized and has hovered around 15,000 annually since 1995.

To provide a sense of the intensity of enforcement, we calculated the risk a marijuana user faces of being arrested for possession. If calculated per joint consumed, the figure nationally is trivial—perhaps one arrest for every 11,000–12,000 joints.[4] However, the relevant risk may be the probability of being arrested during a year of normal consumption. Since mari-

---

[3] These estimates are based on the Treatment Episode Data Set (TEDS), which was started in 1992 and is based on anonymized client-level information for those clients who are publicly funded or those who go to a facility that receives public funding (including those that are privately funded) (HHS, 2009).

[4] Using a national consumption total of 3,500 tons and an average joint of 0.4 grams, we estimate that somewhere on the order of 8.75 billion joints are consumed annually. There are approximately 750,000 possession arrests, generating an average of more than 11,600 joints per arrest.

Figure 2.2
Per Capita Marijuana Arrests in California and the United States, 1990–2008

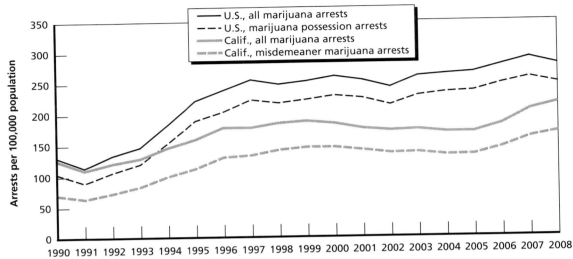

SOURCE: Population figures in the denominator are from the U.S. Census Bureau. U.S. data are from FBI (various years). California data are from CJSC (undated [a], undated [b]).
NOTE: Misdemeanor arrests account for the vast majority of possession arrests in California.

RAND OP315-2.2

juana is mostly consumed by individuals who use it at least once a month,[5] we estimated the risk that such individuals face. We know from prior studies (e.g., Reuter, Hirschfield, and Davies, 2001) that these risks are higher for youth. Table 2.2 presents separate estimates for those aged 12–17 and for the entire population 12 and over. We observe that the annual risk

Table 2.2
Probability of Misdemeanor Marijuana Arrest in California, by Age

Years	Annual Arrest Rate (%)	
	12+ Years Old	12–17 Years Old
2002–2003	2.6	5.4
2003–2004	2.4	4.5
2004–2005	2.4	5.0
2005–2006	2.6	6.1
2006–2007	3.0	6.6

SOURCE: The numerator for these calculations is misdemeanor marijuana arrests (Criminal Justice Statistics Center, undated [b]), and the denominator is the number of past-month marijuana users (SAMHSA, annual). The third column focuses only on juvenile misdemeanor marijuana arrests. Given the aforementioned undercoverage issues associated with NSDUH (i.e., the denominator is too small), these are likely upper-bound estimates.

---

[5]   Kilmer and Pacula (2009) estimate that those who have used in the past 30 days have an annual consumption about ten times as high as those who consume less frequently than every month.

of misdemeanor arrest for those 12–17 (6.6 percent) is more than twice the rate for the full population (3.0 percent).

Arrest is only the first step in the criminal-justice process. To assess the personal consequences of an arrest and estimate the current costs of marijuana enforcement, it is important to have data on the disposition of these arrests. Unfortunately, we are not aware of data on the number of individuals entering probation or local jails as a consequence of arrest for marijuana possession in California. Since state law indicates that those possessing less than 1 ounce are generally supposed to be cited without booking, we can safely infer that most of those arrested for simple possession are not incarcerated at all. For decades now, California law has specified a fine as the maximum penalty. Indeed, when Proposition 36 gave those arrested for simple possession of any drug for the first or second time a treatment alternative to criminal-justice sanctioning, most marijuana arrestees chose not to participate in this diversion program because they already faced so little threat of jailing.[6]

There are approximately 1,500 marijuana prisoners in California (CDCR, 2008a, 2008b), but most felony marijuana offenders in California state courts sentenced to incarceration go to jail, not prison (DOJ, 2004). It is important to note, however, that these felony data do not give a precise picture of the flow of marijuana offenders to jail. They exclude those who are sentenced to jail after a misdemeanor conviction, which might be the result of a plea agreement. They also do not include those who spend time in jail before they are sentenced, which may be a more significant omission (Reuter, Hirschfield, and Davies, 2001; Caulkins, 2010a). There is much more that can be learned about the disposition of marijuana arrests in California.

The Evolving Legal Environment for Marijuana in California

The laws governing the use, production, and distribution of marijuana in California have been in flux for the past 15 years.[7] In 1996, voters passed Proposition 215, which allows medical patients to possess and cultivate marijuana to treat their conditions. Proposition 215 was written in a way that allowed for a broad interpretation of the conditions under which production and distribution were permitted. In 2003, the legislature tried to clarify matters by passing a law known as Chapter 875, which allows any Californian with a doctor's written permission to own as many as six marijuana plants or possess up to half a pound of marijuana.

Over the next seven years, the legal system evolved, often in ways that caused considerable conflict. For example, the California Supreme Court ruled unanimously in 2010 that the legislature's action in 2003 to place limits on the allowed quantities of marijuana (no more than a half a pound) improperly overrode Proposition 215 (*People v. Kelly*, 2010). In addition, not all local governments permitted dispensaries to operate, and those that did frequently changed their policies. For example, Los Angeles saw an explosion in the number of dispensaries. By the end of 2009, it was estimated that about 500–600 dispensaries were operating

---

[6] We do not have the precise figures on the share of marijuana arrestees who rejected their Proposition 36 options or were ineligible, but we know that, for 2005, there were close to 50,000 arrests for marijuana possession in California and fewer than 5,000 Proposition 36 treatment referrals for those with marijuana listed as the primary substance of abuse (50,732 referrals × 71.4 percent of referrals who entered treatment × 12.5 percent—the share of referrals entering treatment who reported marijuana as their primary substance of abuse; Urada et al., 2008).

[7] An excellent account of the situation as it evolved through 2008 is contained in Samuels (2008).

throughout the city of Los Angeles (Hoeffel, 2010). In January 2010, the city council voted to limit the number of dispensaries to 70, and, in May 2010, it warned 439 dispensaries that they must close down in June 2010 (Schwencke and Hoeffel, 2010).

The state now charges a fee to issue a medical-marijuana patient identification card ($66, unless the patient is a Medi-Cal recipient, in which case it is $33); counties can add their own charges. As of June 2010, the state department of public health had issued 42,000 identity cards,[8] and this accounts for only a fraction of individuals who have a physician's recommendation to use marijuana for medicinal purposes. Other regulatory agencies have also had to respond. For example, in March 2009, the California Department of Motor Vehicles changed its rules so participants in the medical-marijuana program could be issued a driver's license; the restrictions imposed were the same faced by any other individual who is prescribed a psychoactive drug.

The federal government under President George W. Bush occasionally raided medical-marijuana dispensaries or growers supplying the dispensaries. In March 2009, the Barack Obama administration announced that it would stop raids on dispensaries that followed state law, although it continues to enforce laws against marijuana production generally.[9]

The existing system is in considerable flux, influenced by the decisions of actors at the local, state, and federal levels. Thus, predicting what will happen with or without legalization is a difficult task.

Marijuana-Related Proposals in California

As of July 2010, there are two marijuana-related bills before the California legislature (Senate Bill [SB] 1449 and Assembly Bill [AB] 2254); in addition, in November 2010, Californians will vote on the proposition known as the Regulate, Control, and Tax Cannabis Act of 2010 (the RCTC proposition).

SB 1449 would not legalize marijuana. Rather, it would reduce the penalty for possessing less than 1 ounce to an infraction—the equivalent of a parking violation—instead of a misdemeanor offense. (To distinguish this from legalization, this is sometimes called depenalization.) In addition to making possession merely an infraction, SB 1449 would eliminate the possibility of booking or court-ordered diversion.[10] The bill passed the Senate on June 3, 2010, and it was voted out of the Assembly's Committee on Public Safety on June 22, 2010. It is now being considered by the full Assembly.

In contrast to SB 1449, AB 2254 and the RCTC proposition would truly legalize marijuana with respect to California, albeit not federal, law, including production and wholesale distribution. It is important to note that no jurisdiction, including the Netherlands, has taken such a step (Reuter, 2010).

---

[8]   These data are drawn from California Department of Health (2010).

[9]   In October 2009, the U.S. Department of Justice published a memorandum for U.S. Attorneys indicating that, "As a general matter, pursuit of these priorities should not focus federal resources in your States on individuals whose actions are in clear and unambiguous compliance with existing state laws providing for the medical use of marijuana."

[10]   The latter is a possibility for those arrested for possession of less than an ounce more than three times in the previous two years.

AB 2254, introduced by Assembly member Tom Ammiano and often referred to as the Ammiano bill, would legalize marijuana for those aged 21 and older and task the Department of Alcoholic Beverage Control (ABC) with regulating its possession, sale, and cultivation. Similar to laws governing alcohol, the bill would require ABC to impose a licensing fee on cultivators and wholesalers that

> will reasonably cover the costs of assuring compliance with the regulations to be issued, but may not exceed five thousand dollars ($5,000) for an initial application, or two thousand five hundred dollars ($2,500) per year for each annual renewal.

The bill would also impose a $50-per-ounce excise tax to be paid at the point of retail (in addition to a sales tax), and it would require that these funds "be expended exclusively for drug education, awareness, and rehabilitation programs under the jurisdiction of the State Department of Alcohol and Drug Programs [ADP]."[11] The bill calls for ADP to annually review whether a lesser excise tax could be charged that would provide sufficient resources for these programs and would give ADP the authority to change the fee.

When the Ammiano bill was introduced in the previous legislative session (as AB 390),[12] BOE (2009b) estimated that it would generate approximately $1.4 billion in tax revenue annually ($990 million from the $50-per-ounce excise tax and $392 million in sales tax revenues).[13] BOE noted that these figures are based on "numerous assumptions,"[14] and it did not describe all of its calculations in detail. There is no mention of the possibility of smuggling or tax evasion or of the nonprice effects that legalization itself could have on consumption because the drug has become legal and more accessible; our analysis shows that these could have an important impact on consumption and public budgets.

The RCTC proposition of 2010 is a voter proposition that will be on the November 2010 ballot (Wheaton, 2009). It would change state law and make it legal for those aged 21 and older to possess, process, share, or transport up to 1 ounce of marijuana and to cultivate plants for personal use in an area that does not exceed a 5-foot–by–5-foot plot, subject to certain limitations, such as not using marijuana on school grounds, while operating a vehicle, or when minors are present. A separate and distinct part of the proposition would allow a city or county to permit, license, and regulate the commercial cultivation, processing, distribution, and sales of marijuana. These latter activities would remain illegal in localities that do not opt in. Hence, personal production, possession, sharing, and use would immediately become legal under state law everywhere in California, but larger-scale production and sale would be legal only in jurisdictions that took additional, local action.

---

[11] The proposed fiscal year (FY) 2010–2011 budget for ADP is close to $600 million (ADP, 2010), and close to half of its budget comes from federal funds.

[12] AB 390 made it out of committee, but the full Assembly did not vote on it before the end of the legislative session.

[13] No mention is made of the projected fees that would be collected from the cultivators and sellers.

[14] Those listed include the following:

> Legalization of marijuana would cause its street price to decline by 50 percent; This 50 percent decline in price would lead to additional consumption of 40 percent; The imposition of the $50/ounce tax would then lead to reduced consumption of 11 percent. . . . Some of the revenue raised would result from additional residents consuming marijuana ([who] were not doing so when it was prohibited by law) in response to being legalized.

However, it unclear whether this language was incorporated into the analysis and, if so, at what level.

Unlike the Ammiano bill, the RCTC proposition does not specify any tax on marijuana, although it would allow *local* governments to establish taxes and fees. It is not clear whether state taxes would be allowed.[15] The California Legislative Analyst's Office (LAO) (Taylor and Genest, 2009) notes that there is "significant uncertainty" about revenues and expenditures from the RCTC proposition. A large amount of the uncertainty comes from the fact that marijuana will still be illegal under federal law. As for major fiscal effects, the LAO reports that there will be

> [s]avings of up to several tens of millions of dollars annually to state and local governments on the costs of incarcerating and supervising certain marijuana offenders; and unknown but potentially major tax, fee, and benefit assessment revenues to state and local government related to the production and sale of marijuana products.

Putting the Proposed Legislation into Context: Some Thoughts from an International Perspective

In recent decades, many countries have implemented legal changes that significantly reduce the extent of criminalization of marijuana use. In some instances, this has reflected a belief that government should not intrude into private life; that was the reasoning of Argentina's Supreme Court of Justice in ruling that possession of any psychoactive drug for personal use could not be prohibited (Cozac, 2009).[16] In other instances, it has been pragmatic, reflecting a belief that criminal penalties are ineffective and intrusive. That was the justification used when Portugal shifted to civil penalties for all drug-possession offenses in 2001 (Hughes and Stevens, 2007). Most changes have reduced the penalties for all psychoactive drugs; only a few countries (Belgium, the Netherlands, and some jurisdictions in Australia and the United States) have singled out marijuana and adopted legislation that removes criminal penalties for possession of that drug only. All but two countries have retained some penalty for marijuana use. Mexico and the Netherlands are the only countries in which it is clear that all penalties for use by adults have been removed.

Only in the Netherlands and Australia have there been any changes in the criminal status of supplying marijuana for nonmedicinal purposes. The Netherlands allows for the sale of small amounts of marijuana (5 grams, about one-sixth of an ounce) through licensed coffee shops. While cultivating and trafficking marijuana are not allowed, police policy is to not arrest individuals with five or fewer plants in their homes ("Netherlands Court," 2008). In four Australian jurisdictions, the penalty for cultivating a very small number of marijuana plants is confiscation and a fine. However, selling marijuana is still subject to criminal penalties (Cam-

---

[15] State marijuana taxes are not allowed by Section 11302 or elsewhere in the RCTC proposition itself, but the purposes articulated in the preamble include "to generate billions of dollars for our *state* and local governments" [emphasis added], and Section 5 allows the state to pass laws that establish a statewide regulatory system for a commercial cannabis industry "to further the purpose of the Act." Presumably, the courts would have to decide whether the ability to establish a regulatory system implies the ability to tax. Even if the state cannot levy marijuana-specific taxes, it could collect the standard sales tax on legal marijuana sales, as well as income tax revenues from marijuana-industry employees whose activities would no longer be under the table.

[16] There have been similar court rulings in Alaska (*Ravin v. State*, 1975; *Noy v. State*, 2003) for modest quantities of cannabis.

eron and Williams, 2001). Thus, in neither of those countries is it legal to both produce and sell marijuana, which would be the case under the Ammiano bill and the RCTC proposition.

It is also important to point out that in no Western country is a user at much risk of being criminally penalized for using marijuana. The rates of arrest for past-year marijuana users in Western countries are typically less than or equal to 3 percent (Kilmer, 2002; Room et al., 2010). More important, almost none of those convicted of simple possession is incarcerated or receives a fine exceeding $1,000 (Pacula, MacCoun, et al., 2005).

Thus, the relaxations in policy so far, with the exception of those in the Netherlands, have not been very significant in terms of reducing the legal risks marijuana users face, particularly when compared to a change like legalization. It is perhaps not surprising, then, that the changes in prevalence of use associated with these previous policy changes have also been very modest (Pacula, 2010b). In short, what is being contemplated in California would go well beyond the Dutch "de facto" legalization of small-quantity transactions. In no country is it completely legal to produce, sell, and use marijuana irrespective of quantity (Reuter, 2010).

CHAPTER THREE

How to Project the Effects of Marijuana Legalization

Building a Logic Model

As mentioned earlier, projecting the effects of legalizing marijuana on use and on tax revenues hinges on estimates of current consumption, current and future prices, how responsive use is to price changes (its "elasticity"), taxes levied and possibly evaded, and the aggregation of many nonprice effects (such as the elimination of any lawbreaking in consuming marijuana). Each of these components, or parameters, of the model is interesting in its own right and, thus, is discussed here before being combined in the next chapter to produce a base-case model estimate. Building such a logic model is critical not only in building the production model but also in ensuring that we have systematically examined all the potential factors that may affect outcomes. The exercise itself often identifies connections that are not intuitively obvious but turn out to be very important.

Figure 3.1 presents a diagram—what is known as a *logic model*—showing how marijuana legalization could influence marijuana consumption and public budgets in California. The boxes in the far left corners represent the government's decision to legalize, tax, and regulate marijuana, and the black boxes capture our main outcomes of interest in this study: consumption and the net effect on state and local budgets. The other boxes and arrows (labeled with letters) demonstrate the various ways legalization can influence these outcomes. Boxes for tax revenues from legal sales and other factors that influence the budgets (besides legal marijuana sales) are gray to highlight that they are important intermediate outcomes to the final budget figures.

Starting at the top left of the figure, legalization will remove the penalties for selling and possessing marijuana. Doing so will immediately lower production and distribution costs (indicated by arrow c); indeed, an important share of the price currently paid for marijuana comes from having to compensate suppliers for participating in a black market and for the inefficiencies created by having to operate covertly (Reuter and Kleiman, 1986; Caulkins and Reuter, 1998, 2010). Post-legalization, users will no longer face this enforcement "tax." Additionally, prices may fall because of shifts in production techniques (e.g., larger and more-efficient plots) and advances in production and processing technologies (Caulkins, 2010b). There are many ways that legalization could influence consumption besides through its effect on price. The reductions in legal penalties are obvious, but there are other mechanisms, including advertising, a change in social norms, availability, and perceived harmfulness (MacCoun, 1993, 2010b; Pacula, 2010b); these are represented by arrow b in the figure.

At the bottom left of the figure, we show that legalizing marijuana will require decisions about the regulatory regime and the tax rate, if any, and these decisions may vary considerably

Figure 3.1
How Marijuana Legalization Could Influence Consumption and State and Local Budgets

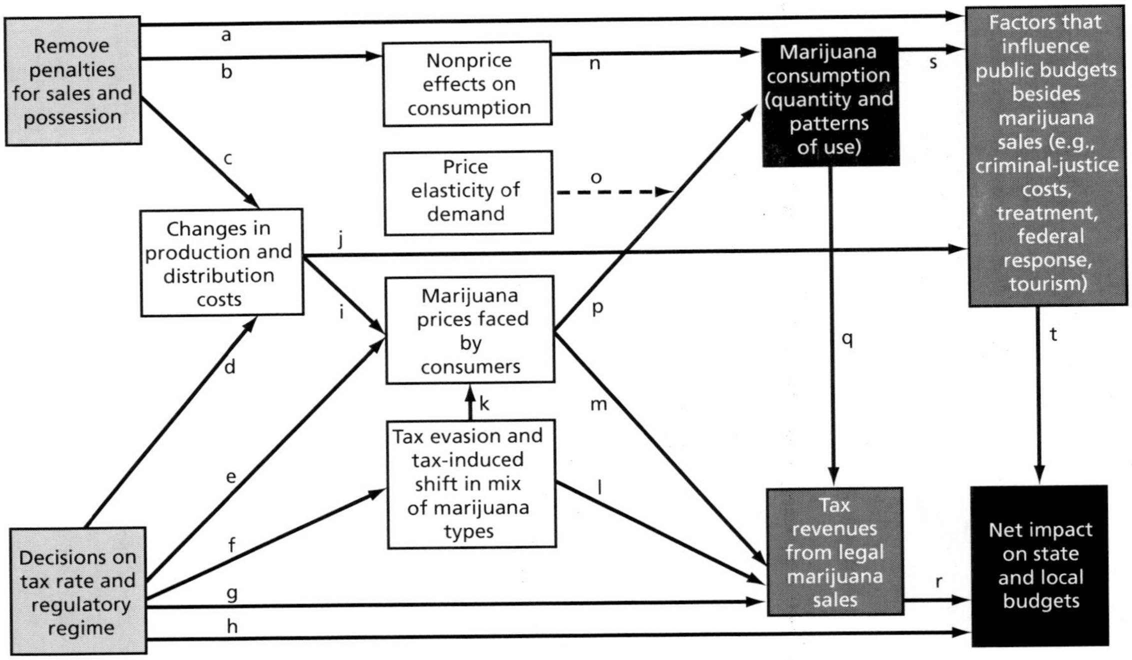

RAND OP315-3.1

by jurisdiction, since the RCTC proposition gives discretion to the county and municipal governments. There are five arrows coming from the box in the bottom left, and we discuss them in a counterclockwise manner. Since it costs money to regulate and collect taxes, there is a direct link between the light-gray box and black budget box (h). Setting the tax rate also obviously influences tax revenues directly (g), but taxes can also elicit a behavioral response (f), including both tax evasion (purchasing untaxed marijuana from the "gray" market) and a shift in the mix of types of marijuana consumed; a fixed excise tax per ounce may give users an incentive to shift to smaller quantities of higher-potency forms of marijuana. For marijuana purchased in the legal market, tax rates also directly influence the prices faced by consumers (e). The regulation of the industry will also influence the production and distribution costs (d).

The arrows pointing to the marijuana-consumption box come from these nonprice effects (n) and from price (p). The impact of price on consumption (p) will depend not only on how much legalization influences price (e, i, k) but also on how sensitive users and potential users are to price (o; represented by the arrow coming from the price-elasticity-of-demand box).

The story gets even more complex when thinking about tax revenues from marijuana sales. Revenues will obviously be influenced by the tax rate (g), consumption (q), and price (through the sales tax) (m), but we must also consider the role of tax evasion (l). Tax evasion influences both tax revenues and the average price paid by consumers (k). If the gray-market price (the price for untaxed marijuana) is substantially different from the prices charged in the legal market, this evasion-induced price decrease could lead to a further increase in consumption.

The gray box at the top right corner represents the factors that could influence state and local budgets besides tax revenue from legal sales. These would include changes in government expenditures on law enforcement (a), changes in government expenditures on drug treatment, or tax revenues from other goods that are purchased (or not purchased) because of a change in marijuana consumption and production (j, s; e.g., bongs, fertilizer, alcohol). This box would include the impacts of tourism, and it also captures the possibility of a federal intervention (e.g., making federal highway funds contingent on states not legalizing marijuana—similar to what was done to make sure all states imposed a legal drinking age of 21 years). Both of these possibilities are addressed in Chapter Four. It is this box (t) in combination with tax revenues (r) and the regulation costs (h) that generate the net impact on state and local budgets.

In the rest of this chapter, we provide further insight into the key parameters needed to project the effect on marijuana consumption and tax revenues from marijuana sales. In Chapter Five, we discuss some other possible ways in which marijuana legalization could affect state and local budgets.

Current Price

We need an estimate of the current price because economists typically project price-induced changes in consumption by multiplying the percentage change in price by the elasticity of demand, or percentage change in consumption per 1-percent change in price. (This is discussed in detail later in this chapter.) The percentage change in price is computed as the difference between the projected post-legalization price and the current price.

There are many types of marijuana, mostly reflecting differences in the amount of delta-9-tetrahydrocannabinol, or THC, which determines the intoxication potential. Also, the price per unit weight varies with quantity purchased—that is, there are "quantity discounts" (Caulkins and Padman, 1993). Here and throughout this paper, we define *price* as the price of an ounce of marijuana that has THC content comparable to that of sinsemilla today and that is both unbranded and unbundled. That price is currently $300–$450 per ounce in California (Bond and Caulkins, 2010).[1] We focus on the price of sinsemilla-grade marijuana because it constitutes a substantial share of domestic production in California today—and would likely predominate in the legalization scenarios we believe most likely (grow house–, not farm field–, based production).

Post-legalization, some suppliers may seek to differentiate their marijuana through branding, advertising, or some sort of quality difference not related to intoxication potential. *Unbundled* refers to marijuana sold as marijuana (as opposed to marijuana-impregnated brownies, beer, or other products) to be consumed off-premises (akin to the grocery-store price of beer rather than the price of beer in a bar). The price of beer or, possibly in the future, marijuana purchased for consumption in a bar or restaurant includes the cost of the rent, utilities, wait staff's wages, and such, which are bundled together with the price of the beer or marijuana itself.

---

[1] According to the Drug Enforcement Administration, "[s]insemilla, in Spanish, means without seed. Growing the female cannabis plant separate from the male cannabis plant prevents pollination, resulting in an increase in THC (tetrahydrocannabinol) levels and bud growth" (NIDC, 2001).

Current Consumption

To project consumption changes in percentage terms, one needs to know the current level of consumption. The higher the current quantity consumed, the greater the projected tax revenues from legalizing and taxing marijuana. A number of studies across different countries have found that total consumption divided by the number of past-year users is close to 100 grams, or a little less than 4 ounces.[2] Based on the available data,[3] it seems reasonable that between 400 and 500 metric tons (MT) of marijuana are consumed in California each year. Although it is unknown how BOE (2009b) generated its estimate of 454 MT, that figure is consistent with the ranges calculated here and by Gieringer (2009). And, given that some readers may want to compare our revenue estimates with those of BOE, we use 454 MT in our base calculations.[4] To generate national consumption estimates, we multiply the California estimate by the total number of marijuana users in the United States divided by the number of marijuana users in California.[5]

In our model, we convert these total quantities into sinsemilla-equivalent quantities, adjusting for THC content. For example, we count 2.5 grams of commercial-grade marijuana with 40 percent of the potency of sinsemilla as equivalent to 1 gram of sinsemilla. Consumption totals are reported based on the current mix (so they are directly comparable to the 454-MT figure), and changes are reported as changes in "sinsemilla-equivalent quantities" (effectively, changes in THC consumption); however, the tax projections allow for the possibility that the mix of marijuana types may shift toward higher-potency forms.

Future Price

No modern nation has ever legalized commercial marijuana production, so there are literally no relevant data to guide estimates of marijuana-production costs after legalization. Although

---

[2]   Bouchard (2008) calculates that past-year users in Quebec used, on average, 94 grams in 2003 and notes that this is consistent with studies from other countries. He raises the possibility of a "100 grams-per-user benchmark." Kilmer and Pacula's (2009) estimate for the United States is strikingly similar (93 grams), as is Slack et al.'s (2008) New Zealand figure of 98 grams. The United Nations Office on Drugs and Crime (UNODC) (2006) classifies marijuana users into four groups (casual, regular, daily, and chronic users) and presents their prevalence as well as expected annual consumption based on an international review of the literature; the weighted average for any past-year user is 116 grams per annum.

[3]   Little has been written about the total quantity of marijuana consumed in California. Gieringer (2009), using data from NSDUH and assumptions about quantity consumed, suggests that Californians consume 431–499 MT of marijuana annually. BOE (2009b) assumes that Californians consume 454 MT annually, although it gives no supporting information about how this number was generated. (BOE notes only that "Our literature review indicates that estimated consumption of marijuana in California amounts to one million pounds per year, or 16 million ounces.") The 2006–2007 NSDUH (SAMHSA, 2007) reports that 3,342,000 Californians used marijuana in the previous year. If we apply Kilmer and Pacula's (2009) assumption that 20 percent of surveyed marijuana users deny their marijuana use, that suggests a rough estimate of 4.2 million past-year users in California. Using the estimate of 93 grams per past-year user from Kilmer and Pacula and the 116 grams from UNODC generates a range of 391–487 MT.

[4]   An important contribution to this estimate would be an estimate of the share of marijuana users not covered by NSDUH. NSDUH was redesigned in the early 2000s partly to decrease undercoverage.

[5]   The assumption that quantity consumed per user in California is the same as it is throughout the country could be revisited in future analyses. Other estimates for annual U.S. consumption range from 1,000 MT (Abt Associates, 2001) to nearly 10,000 MT (Gettman, 2007), with estimates from the DEA and UNODC hovering around 4,200 MT (Drug Availability Steering Committee, 2002; UNODC, 2005).

the Dutch have essentially legalized retail distribution, they have not legalized production. The same could be said about California's medicinal-marijuana policy; large-scale production for wholesale purposes is not legal, and, at any rate, quality standards and regulatory oversight are likely to be different for recreational than for medicinal marijuana. Relying primarily on the gray literature (e.g., textbooks on marijuana production), some interviews, and, where possible, the scientific literature, we created cost estimates for four different production methods, which, in decreasing order of cost, are (1) private hydroponic homegrown on a 5-foot–by–5-foot area; (2) filling most of a 1,500-square-foot residential house with intensive hydroponic production (with artificial lights, best practices, and so on); (3) growing marijuana in "greenhouse farms"; and (4) unfettered outdoor farming that achieves efficiencies of the sort that American agriculture achieves when growing tomatoes, lettuce, or asparagus. Our estimation method is akin to what an entrepreneur would use when developing a business plan for a new product or production process.

For our model, we take the second method as the base case (filling most of a 1,500-square-foot residential house) on the grounds that the third and fourth might attract federal enforcement attention. However, even when factoring in the cost of artificial lighting, rent for a house (which is much more expensive than for a greenhouse), and other expenses, post-legalization house-based production costs would still only be on the order of $300–$400 per pound, including harvest and processing (Caulkins, 2010b), or only about one-tenth of the current wholesale price. There are several reasons to anticipate such a sharp decline. First, we anticipate that workers' wages will fall because employers will not have to pay a risk premium to employees for participating in an illegal activity.[6] Second, there will be greater ability to use labor-saving automation, especially in the manicuring stage. Third, production at the level of an entire grow house, or several houses operated together, permits economies of scale not available to grows kept small enough to avoid attracting the attention of not just federal but also local law enforcement. Fourth, assuming that growers avoid attracting federal law-enforcement attention, they will face minimal risk of arrest and forfeiture.

In our base case, we assume typical producer and retailer markups of 25 percent and 33 percent,[7] respectively, and allow an additional $40 per pound for logistics and distribution, suggesting an untaxed legal retail price of about $38 per ounce (see Caulkins, 2010b). Thus, key drivers of retail price will include whether an excise tax is imposed (e.g., the Ammiano bill's proposal of $50 per ounce), whether such a tax is successfully collected or evaded, and whether regulatory and compliance burdens create substantial deadweight costs on producers and distributors. These are naturally very hard to predict, so we provide projections conditional on assumptions about these factors.

Figure 3.2 displays the components of the taxed, legal price, assuming a $50-per-ounce excise tax with indoor production in residential houses that are essentially filled with marijuana plants (1,300 out of 1,500 square feet for plants) grown with artificial light, with one

---

[6] For present purposes, we do not need to know what the current hourly wage rates are, but Caulkins (2010b) found a number of statements in the gray literature suggesting that $20 to $25 per hour might not be atypical of cash payments to people who had no ownership stake in the grow. By way of contrast, agricultural workers in California harvesting and tending legal crops typically cost the employer no more than $10, including whatever benefits are (or are not) provided. For example, O*NET OnLine (2008) cites an average wage for California nursery and greenhouse laborers of $8.60 per hour.

[7] These appear to be typical markups for agricultural and retail operations, respectively (Caulkins, 2010b).

Figure 3.2
Components of the Taxed, Legal Price Under Base-Case
Assumptions

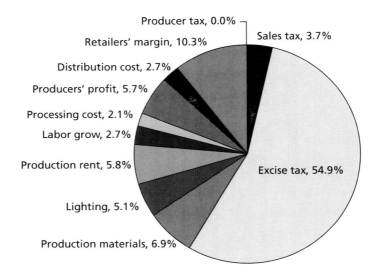

SOURCE: Caulkins (2010b).
NOTE: Assumes a $50-per-ounce excise tax.
RAND OP315-3.2

full-time agricultural worker per house.[8] The excise tax would account for more than half the retail price. Production and processing costs and profits account for a bit less than 30 percent of the cost structure, with the biggest components being materials (6.9 percent, mostly growing medium and consumables); house rent (5.8 percent); producers' markup, including profit (5.7 percent); electricity for lighting (5.1 percent), and labor (4.8 percent, very roughly evenly divided between growing and the harvesting and processing). The remaining chunk stems from distribution and retail costs (and profits).

Tax Rate and Evasion

The average retail price paid will depend on what taxes are imposed and collected. The RCTC proposition does not mention any specific tax rate, leaving it to the discretion of the local governments. Obviously, that makes it extraordinarily difficult to forecast what tax revenues will be. As a base case, we consider a uniform $50-per-ounce excise tax throughout the state. We do this for the sake of comparability with others' estimates (e.g., those based on the Ammiano bill), although there is no particular reason to think that $50 per ounce will be the tax rate if the RCTC proposition passes, and there is even some reason to doubt that a uniform high tax would be sustainable unless it were imposed at the state level.

Just because an excise tax is levied does not mean that it will be collected. In this regard, findings from the tobacco experience are particularly relevant. In the early 1990s, various Canadian provinces tried imposing cigarette taxes on the order of $3 per pack but had to

---

[8]   For more details, see Caulkins (2010b).

repeal them because a black market of untaxed cigarettes quickly emerged that accounted for perhaps 30 percent of sales (Joossens and Raw, 2000; Non-Smokers' Rights Association, 2009). There is sharp disagreement in the literature about the extent of tobacco tax evasion. To generalize and simplify, public-health researchers downplay the extent of smuggling; for example, Alamar, Mahmoud, and Glantz (2003) estimate that, in California, only 1–4.2 percent of cigarettes are smuggled to evade excise taxes. In contrast, BOE (1999a) estimates that 12–27 percent of cigarettes in California are sold without payment of excise taxes.

An important concern is that the proposed $50-per-ounce marijuana excise tax would be much higher than state tobacco taxes, which are all below $5 per ounce (LaFaive et al., 2008). LaFaive et al.'s (2008) data on cigarette excise taxes and evasion suggest that states with higher excise taxes have higher rates of tax evasion. Indeed, if their estimated evasion rates are correct, then extrapolating the resulting positive relationship between tobacco tax rates and tax evasion to the $50-per-ounce level would suggest that evasion would be (much more than) complete, and no taxes would be collected at all. Further, leaving aside the tobacco analogy, the financial reward for evading the Ammiano-bill (or $50-per-ounce) tax on a pound of marijuana after legalization will be greater than the financial reward is today for smuggling 1 pound of marijuana from Mexico into California, since the price of a pound of Mexican marijuana in California today is less than $800 (Caulkins, Morris, and Ratnatunga, 2010).

While the tax per unit weight is the obvious metric in terms of the challenge of covert smuggling, it is not the only relevant metric, and a $50-per-ounce tax is high but not unprecedented in terms of cost per year for the average user or as a percentage of plausible retail prices, as is suggested by Table 3.1.

Changes in the Mix of Types of Marijuana

Marijuana is consumed in many different forms that vary in THC content, ranging from commercial grade (low potency) to domestic midgrade to high-grade sinsemilla (higher potency), as well other variants. The price per gram is roughly proportional to the THC content (Gieringer, 1994). For example, DEA data show that sinsemilla has about 2.4 times the potency and is a little more than twice as expensive per unit weight as commercial grade (NIDA, 2008). A tax assessed on the weight of marijuana (e.g., $50 per ounce) is higher in terms of dollars per unit of THC or per hour of intoxication for lower-potency forms than for higher-potency forms. (An alternative taxation strategy would be to place a tax on the THC itself [and, possibly, regulate its ratio to cannabidiol and other components] to discourage the production of more-potent marijuana products; MacCoun, 2010a). Thus, the Ammiano bill's proposed tax gives users an incentive to switch to higher-potency forms, a trend that would be reinforced if, as in our base-case scenario, legal production takes place primarily in grow houses.

That change would have no important effect on sales tax revenues inasmuch as prices are proportional to THC content, but it could substantially reduce excise revenues. In particular, actual excise revenues would equal the more-simplistic prediction—one that fails to consider the changing mix—multiplied by an adjustment factor that is equal to the average THC potency before legalization divided by the average THC potency after legalization. For example, if there were only two types of marijuana, commercial grade and sinsemilla, if sinsemilla were 2.4 times as potent, and if legalization changed the mix from 20 percent sinsemilla

Table 3.1
How One Contemplated Marijuana Excise Tax Compares to Some Other Familiar or Proposed Excise Taxes

Feature	Marijuana	Cigarettes	Beer	80-Proof Distilled Spirits	Soda Pop	Gasoline
Unit base for taxation	Ounce	Pack	Gallon	Gallon	Ounce	Gallon
State or local excise tax ($)	50	0.87	0.20	3.30	0.01	0.466
Federal excise tax ($)	0	1.01	0.48	10.80	0	0.184
Total excise taxes ($)	50	1.88	0.78	14.10	0.01	0.65
Specific gravity	0.235	0.235	1.05	0.92	1.03	0.739
Grams per unit	28.35	20	3,974.7	3,482.6	30.46	2,797.4
Cubic centimeters per unit	120.49	85	3,785.4	3,785.4	29.57	3,785.4
Tax per gram ($)	1.76	0.09	0.0002	0.0040	0.0003	0.0002
Tax per cubic centimeter ($)	0.41	0.02	0.0002	0.0037	0.0003	0.0002
Basis for retail price, with taxes	Guess of $50/oz. untaxed	Midrange from casual Internet search	$6 for 6-pack of 12-oz. cans	$25 for 750-ml bottle	$1.49 for 2-liter bottle untaxed	$3.11/gal. state average
Approximate retail price, with taxes ($)	100	4	10.67	126.18	2.17	3.11
Tax as percentage of total, with taxes	50	47	7	11	31	21
Daily consumption for typical daily user	1 g.	1 pack	2 12-oz. cans	2 1-oz. shots	2 16-oz. servings	10,000 miles/year at 25 mpg
Annual tax burden for typical daily user ($)	644	685	53	80	117	260

to 90 percent sinsemilla, then, because of quality switching, excise tax revenues would be more than 40 percent smaller than would be predicted by a model that did not allow for switching. [9]

How Price Changes Affect Use: The Elasticity of Demand

There is a substantial and fairly high-quality academic literature that empirically estimates how responsive drug use is to price changes (Pacula, Grossman, et al., 2001; DeSimone and Farrelly, 2003; Pacula, Chriqui, and King, 2003; Zhao and Harris, 2004; Williams et al., 2004; van Ours and Williams, 2007; Clements and Zhao, 2009). Disappointingly, the marijuana studies are weaker than studies of both licit substances (such as alcohol and tobacco) and some illegal drugs (such as cocaine). The explanation is that, for various technical reasons, price data are scarcer and more complicated for marijuana than for cocaine.

The marijuana literature is strongest on measuring the "participation" elasticity, meaning how price changes affect the number of users. A typical finding is that a 10-percent fall in price will increase the number of users by about 3 percent, implying a participation elasticity of $(3\%/-10\%) = -0.3$. However, to project tax revenues and some health consequences, we want the effect of price on the *total quantity consumed*, not on the *number of users*. The reason is that some people who would have used anyway might use more if the price falls. There are no truly satisfying estimates of this "total price elasticity" in the marijuana literature. For tobacco, the total elasticity is roughly 1.5 or 2 times as large as the participation elasticity (Harris and Chan, 1999; Chaloupka and Grossman, 1996; Hu et al., 1995; Lewit and Coate, 1981). Thus, in the absence of marijuana-specific information, we multiply our participation elasticity of -0.3 by 1.75 to proxy the total elasticity. After accounting for possible income effects, we settle on a baseline total price elasticity of -0.54.[10]

Nonprice Effects on Consumption from Both Legalization and Promotion

There are many mechanisms by which a change in marijuana laws or their enforcement might influence drug use, including changes in legal risks, employer risks (through drug testing), price and availability, and social attitudes and norms (MacCoun and Reuter, 2001). Unfortunately, we do not know enough about each mechanism to specify the relative importance of each one; thus, we cannot specify the net impact with any confidence.

Empirically, there are case studies that provide relevant evidence: (1) U.S. and international experience with the depenalization of cannabis use; (2) the Alaska and South Australia home-cultivation experience; (3) the effect of increasing the legal drinking age in U.S. states;

---

[9]
$$\text{Adjustment multiplier} - \frac{0.2 \times 2.4 + (1 - 0.2)}{0.9 \times 2.4 + (1 - 0.9)} = 0.566.$$

[10] Especially for heavy users, a price decline acts almost like an increase in income because it allows the person to afford the same quantities of everything he or she had been buying before (marijuana and other goods), plus some more. Based on our analysis of NSDUH, we estimate that the median gram of marijuana is consumed by someone who spends about 5 percent of income on marijuana. So, for a typical user, a 70-percent price decline would feel like a 3.5-percent increase in income, perhaps leading to an extra ("income elasticity") bump up of 3.5 percent in use. Hence, our base-case total elasticity is $-0.3 \times 1.75 \times 1.035 = -0.54$.

and (4) the Dutch cannabis coffee-shop experience. However, none of these case studies is directly analogous to full-scale regulated legalization—even the Dutch maintain a prohibition on high-level cannabis trafficking and large-scale production—and none appears to involve a drop in prices of the magnitude that could occur under full legalization. Still, we think that the case studies provide some basis for a rough estimate of the nonprice effects of legalization. In a forthcoming analysis, MacCoun (2010b) assesses what we can learn from each of these experiences based on the available evidence.

Correctly identifying causal impact is difficult, but, together, these case studies suggest that cannabis legalization would plausibly lead to increases in consumption, above and beyond those from price drops. If we attribute the largest estimated effects exclusively to the policies (a controversial but cautious assumption), then the Dutch experience suggests a temporary increase of around 35 percent in past-month prevalence. The Alaska and South Australian experiences and the change in the drinking age suggest smaller effects, but these were less dramatic changes than found in the Dutch experience. (For more information, see MacCoun, 2010c.) Taken together, the available evidence suggests that the nonprice impact on consumption might be on the order of a 35-percent increase in past-month use. Given the ambiguity and noisiness of the data, estimates in the range of 5 to 50 percent seem plausible.

Starting Values for the Base-Case Scenario

Table 3.2 provides a summary of the values we use for our base scenario. None of these estimates should be viewed as being in any way precise, but our judgment, analyses, and read of the evidence suggest that these are reasonable starting values.

Table 3.2
Base-Case Values for Some Key Parameters

Parameter	Base Value
Prelegalization	
Retail price ($)	375
Total amount consumed in California per year	1 million pounds (454 MT)
Price elasticity of demand (participation)	–0.3
Elasticity of demand (total)	–0.54
Post-legalization	
Tax per ounce ($)	50
Wholesale price ($)	26
Gray-market price ($)	68
Legal, untaxed ($)	38
Legal, taxed (with excise and sales taxes) ($)	91
Nonprice effect of legalization on consumption (%)	35
Increase in average potency of marijuana (determines the excise tax adjustment) (%)	77 (i.e., marijuana after legalization has 1.77 times as much THC, on average)
Evasion rate	Unknown (used a sensitivity parameter)

NOTE: All prices are for 1 oz. of sinsemilla that is neither branded nor bundled.

Projections with a $50-per-Ounce Tax

This chapter describes our base-case estimates for the effect of marijuana legalization with a $50-per-ounce tax on marijuana consumption in California and tax revenues from those marijuana sales. We highlight two distinct types of uncertainty in the projections: parameter uncertainty and structural uncertainty. *Parameter uncertainty* relates to the value of quantitative model inputs, such as those listed in Table 3.2 in Chapter Three. *Structural uncertainty* speaks more to the assumptions underlying the model, such as the shape of the demand curve or whether marijuana exported from California will be taxed.

To demonstrate how much parameter uncertainty can influence projections, we begin by fixing the values for all the parameters except one: the proportion of marijuana consumed in California on which tax is not collected, either because it is homegrown or because it is purchased from the tax-evading gray market. As noted in Chapter Two, the RCTC proposition does not specify a tax rate. It also does not specify a particular regulatory regime, which could influence the probability of evasion as well.[1] In theory, this evasion rate could range from 0 to 100 percent, with the latter implying that the state would not generate any tax revenue from marijuana sales. Since there is essentially no empirical basis for predicting the actual rate, we present the results for the full range of evasion rates, represented on the horizontal or x-axis in Figure 4.1.

To demonstrate how structural uncertainty can influence projections, we include two panels in Figure 4.1, each of which makes a different assumption about the shape of the demand curve for marijuana. Demand curves tell us how much of a good will be consumed at any given price; however, we have evidence concerning the demand curve's shape over the range of prices observed over only the past 30 years or so, and legalization would push prices down to levels not seen in that period.[2] Here, we consider two demand curves that are often assumed in elementary economic analyses (linear and constant elasticity demand), but we

---

[1] In this chapter, we also consider small-scale home production (≤5' × 5' plot) as a type of tax evasion.

[2] For those familiar with analysis of the Challenger space shuttle disaster, this issue is similar to data about the relationship between O-ring performance and temperature. The launch temperature on January 27, 1986, was "beyond the support of the historical data" (to use the technical jargon). Simply put, all the evidence about O-ring damage came from temperatures of 53° F and above, whereas the forecast temperature was 26–29° F (Tufte, 1997; Robison et al., 2002). Likewise, all our evidence about marijuana demand comes from times when average wholesale sinsemilla prices were above $3,000 per pound (inflation-adjusted to today's dollars), but we expect post-legalization prices to be much lower, perhaps something on the order of $350 × (1 + 25%) = $440 per pound.

Figure 4.1
Assumptions About the Demand Curve and the Rate of Tax Evasion Greatly Affect Projections

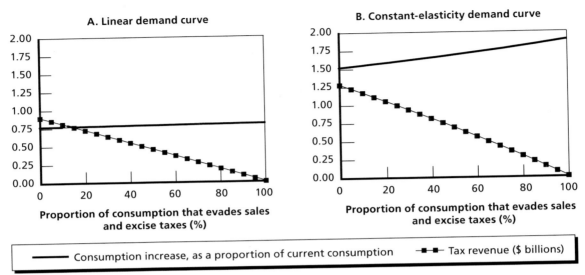

NOTE: This pair of charts shows how consumption and tax revenues are affected by the rate of tax evasion (indicated by the horizontal axis) and the shape of the demand curve (one panel for each of two shapes), while holding all other assumptions constant. For the marked line, the y-axis represents tax revenue in terms of billions of dollars (1.00 = $1 billion). For the solid line, the y-axis represents the percentage increase in consumption (1.00 = 100% increase). If there were no tax evasion (far left or 0% on the horizontal axis), legalization would increase consumption by 76% if demand was linear (panel A) and by 151% if demand had a constant elasticity, which implies a certain kind of curvature (panel B). (The 151% can be read from where the solid line in panel B touches the vertical axis.)

RAND OP315-4.1

have no reason to believe that either is correct.[3] We use the curves because they are familiar (at least to economists) and illustrate how consequential such seemingly innocuous assumptions can be, not because we believe one or the other is in any sense preferred. We also stress that demand-curve shape is by no means the only structural assumption embedded in our model. We consider the importance of some other structural assumptions in Chapter Six.

The left panel of Figure 4.1 shows the model's projection of consumption and tax revenue as a function of the evasion rate, assuming a linear demand curve. Naturally, when the evasion rate is 100 percent, the state does not collect any tax revenue. At the other extreme, with no tax evasion, we assume that, for every ounce, users will pay $38 (pretax price) plus an additional 9-percent sales tax ($3.40 per ounce) and a $50-per-ounce excise tax, for a total retail price of $91 per ounce.

As discussed earlier, it is important to consider how legalization could influence the type of marijuana being consumed. At the aforementioned price of $91 per ounce, we project total consumption in California to increase by about 76 percent, to what would be 800 MT if there were no change in the mix of types of marijuana. Multiplying this 800 MT by $50 per ounce gives an estimate of state excise tax revenues of $1.4 billion, but the mix change is projected to reduce that by about 43 percent, to $0.8 billion. Multiplying 800 MT by a $3.40-per-ounce

---

[3] With a linear demand curve, the slope is constant but the price elasticity of demand is not. That is, the price elasticity of demand is not constant at all points on the curve. With the constant-elasticity demand curve, the price elasticity of demand is assumed to be the same at each point. (The curve is nonlinear, having the form of a power law.)

sales tax generates another roughly $96 million in tax revenue, so the tax revenue line crosses the vertical or y-axis at $0.9 billion; the sales tax is not affected by the mix change because the price per unit of THC is assumed to be the same across marijuana types. As the evasion rate increases, more individuals face the gray-market price (assumed to be 25 percent lower at $91 × 0.75 = $68 per ounce), and the total amount of marijuana consumed increases. In the 100-percent-evasion scenario, we would expect the total consumption to increase by 79 percent, slightly more than the 76 percent at 0-percent evasion.

The right panel of Figure 4.1 presents the same information, but this time for the constant-elasticity demand model. Once again, we see the expected decrease in revenues as a function of evasion, but it is not quite a straight line because consumption increases slightly more than linearly given the amount of evasion. When the evasion rate is 0 percent, this model projects the increase in total consumption to be 151 percent. This is roughly double the equivalent increase with a linear demand curve because of the underlying assumption about how consumption responds to price changes that go outside prices observed in historical data. The difference between the two consumption projections grows as the evasion rate increases because that increase exacerbates the price decline, reaching a projected 187-percent increase in consumption with 100-percent tax evasion.

Once again, we stress that we do not know what the demand curve for marijuana actually looks like and that neither of the curves shown here may accurately capture that demand. However, contrasting results with these two demand curves highlights the fact that a change in just one structural assumption can have a large impact on projected consumption and revenue.

The calculations just discussed used a single value for each of the model parameters listed in Table 3.2 in Chapter Three besides the tax-evasion rates. Since none of those other parameters is known with certainty, readers should actually think of each point on each line in Figure 4.1 as being surrounded by a range or distribution of higher or lower values that could result from uncertainty in these other parameters' values. In Figure 4.2, we illustrate the uncertainty that comes from not knowing these other parameter values with certainty by showing the distributions surrounding the estimates for one specific tax-evasion rate (25 percent), while still assuming a $50-per-ounce tax. Figure 4.1 has four estimates corresponding to a 25-percent tax-evasion rate: changes in consumption and in tax revenues for both the linear and the constant-elasticity demand curve. Hence, Figure 4.2 displays four distributions in the form of box-and-whisker plots.[4]

The bottom and top of each box in Figure 4.2 show the range of values necessary to capture half of the probability distribution. For example, the leftmost box shows that, when the demand curve is assumed to be linear, the tax is $50 per ounce, tax-evasion rate is 25 percent, and supply is assumed to be infinitely elastic, our model suggests that, 50 percent of the time, the increase in consumption will range from 75 to 98 percent (the 25th and 75th percentiles,

---

[4] Values for the other parameters are selected using a method called Monte Carlo simulation and, more specifically, a *triangle distribution*, meaning that the values can be anywhere within their specified ranges, but values near the base-case value (from Table 5.1 in Chapter Five) are most likely. Ranges for some of the important parameters are as follows: current price = $300–450 per ounce; current California consumption = 400–500 MT; demand elasticity = −0.4 −−1.26 (composed of several subcalculations); wholesale price = $15–38 per ounce; nonprice effect of legalization on consumption = 5–50%; potency adjustment = 1.57 − 1.97.

Figure 4.2
Illustration of Uncertainty About Legalization's Effect on Marijuana Consumption and Tax Revenues from Marijuana Sales with a $50-per-Ounce Excise Tax

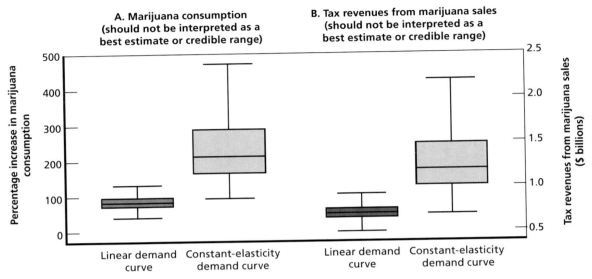

NOTE: This figure is intended to highlight the uncertainty associated with projecting marijuana consumption and tax revenues post-legalization. It should not be interpreted as a best estimate or credible range. The figure varies parameters listed in Table 3.2 in Chapter Three, while holding constant the excise tax (at $50 per ounce) and tax evasion rate (25 percent), to show how there is actually a distribution of values around each point in Figure 4.1. The calculations assume an infinitely elastic supply curve (which is a common assumption but could bias these numbers upward if, in fact, the supply curve is upward sloping). Outside values (i.e., 75th [or 25th] percentile ± 1.5 × interquartile range) are included in the calculations but are not displayed. Results for each demand curve are based on 10,000 runs of a Monte Carlo simulation.

RAND OP315-4-2

respectively). The whiskers indicate a broader range that reflects most of the possible outcomes that are not outsiders.[5]

As we would expect after looking at Figure 4.1, assumptions about the shape of the demand curve matter enormously. People who believe that the demand curve is bowed, as with the constant-elasticity demand model, should expect not only much larger outcomes than people who believe that the demand curve is linear (in terms of both tax revenues and increases in consumption); they also should also expect that it will be far more difficult to pin down what will happen. Their boxes are both higher and more spread out than those associated with the linear demand curve. The 25th and 75th percentiles (represented by the bottom and top of each box in Figure 4.2, respectively) for consumption are 167–289 percent for constant-elasticity demand, much larger and more spread out than the 75–98 percent for the linear demand curve. The equivalent figures for revenues are $0.65 billion to $0.76 billion for linear demand and $1 billion to $1.49 billion for constant-elasticity demand.

We caution readers that these revenue figures being somewhat similar to those reported by BOE is more or less coincidence. BOE neglected tax evasion and changes in potency, while considering only a linear demand curve and one particular elasticity. Those differences more

---

[5]   More specifically, the lines extending from these boxes (the "whiskers") represent the 75th (or 25th) percentile ±1.5 × interquartile range.

or less offset each other when the tax-evasion rate is 25 percent but do not for other rates of tax evasion.

Once again, readers should not interpret our use of these two particular demand curves, the 25-percent evasion rate, or the $50-per-ounce excise tax as signaling what we think the most likely scenario will be. The purpose of Figure 4.2 is only to demonstrate how much additional uncertainty there is about revenue and consumption estimates, above and beyond that already illustrated in Figure 4.1, when one recognizes that none of the other model parameters is known with certainty.

CHAPTER FIVE

Assessing the Projections

In this chapter, we discuss the results of our base-case scenario. In addition to addressing effects on consumption and tax revenues from marijuana sales, we consider other budgetary and nonbudgetary effects.

Consumption Effects

A central question about legalization is whether it will make marijuana consumption go up a little or a lot. The central point of Chapter Four is that it is hard to answer that question because there is great uncertainty about how much consumption will increase. However, it is also hard to answer that question because different people have different thresholds for distinguishing between "a little" and "a lot."

For the sake of exposition, we will consider a doubling in consumption as a bright line for defining whether consumption changes are small or large. This threshold is not entirely arbitrary. It roughly distinguishes between prevalence rates that have and have not been observed in the United States in the past (MacCoun, 2010a).[1] Marijuana use peaked in the United States in 1978–1979, and Table 5.1 shows how past-month use (our best available proxy for consumption) was twice as high in the student and household populations compared to what it was in 2008. The share of high-school seniors using daily was also twice as high (37 percent and 19 percent, respectively).

While the share of past-month users who used daily was similar for 1978 and 2008 (29 percent and 28 percent, respectively, based on dividing data the second row of Table 5.1 by data in the third row), this figure is not constant (e.g., at the midpoint of this series—1993—the corresponding number was closer to 16 percent). We also know that the marijuana seized and analyzed in 1978 was of lower potency than it was in 2008, suggesting that the harms and quantity consumed may not be the same (NIDA, 2008). Nonetheless, we offer this bright line to give readers context about what a doubling in the prevalence rate would look like, not necessarily what the associated costs would be. For the scenario presented in Figure 4.2 in Chapter Four, we found that the proportion of 10,000 trials for which consumption more than doubled was 22.1 percent with linear demand curve and 99.98 percent with constant-elasticity demand curve.

---

[1] In our projection model, consumption is defined in terms of quantity consumed. The increase in the number of users would be smaller, perhaps roughly half as great, as the increase in quantity consumed.

Table 5.1
A 100-Percent Increase in Prevalence Would Bring Us Close to 1978 Levels

Measures	Circa 1978	2008
High-school seniors reporting past-month marijuana use (%)	37.1 (1978)	19.4 (2008)
High-school seniors reporting using marijuana daily for previous month (%)	10.7 (1978)	5.4 (2008)
Household population 12+ reporting past-month marijuana use (%)[a]	13.2 (1979)	6.1 (2008)

SOURCES: Johnston et al. (annual); SAMHSA (annual).

[a] There were methodological changes to the National Household Survey on Drug Abuse (NHSDA) and NSDUH that make comparisons across this period difficult. We include them here for informational purposes.

Budget Effects Beyond Tax Revenues

Legalization will have various fiscal impacts. The goal from a budgeting perspective is not to minimize the cost of regulation but to maximize the tax revenue net of cost of regulation. In this section, we consider the potential effects of legalization on the costs associated with law enforcement, treatment, hospitalizations, and regulation.

Law-Enforcement Costs

Enforcing marijuana laws imposes costs on criminal-justice agencies. It is difficult to estimate these costs because most marijuana arrests are for misdemeanor possession and we do not have good information about the results of misdemeanor arrests specifically for marijuana. We do have better information about felony convictions and terms of incarceration, but, as was made clear in Chapter Two, these are not normal paths for those arrested for marijuana-related offenses.

Previous estimates of the cost of enforcing marijuana laws in California differ by an order of magnitude. Gieringer (2009) estimates the costs to be close to $200 million annually, while Miron (2010) estimates this figure to be closer to $1.9 billion per annum. Interestingly, both of these studies use the same basic approach: prorating of historical costs. An example of how to prorate historical costs is as follows: If the total expenditure on an activity (such as arresting) is $100 million per year and 10 percent of those actions involve marijuana offenders, then the estimate of that component attributable to enforcing marijuana prohibition is $10 million per year.

We use an essentially similar approach obtaining cost and administrative criminal-justice data from local, state, and, sometimes, national sources (for detail, see Caulkins, 2010a). Our analysis accounts for the fact that police do more than just make arrests and applies different costs for misdemeanor and felony offenses. Table 5.2 compares our results with the previous estimates mentioned; we include a separate column for costs specifically for offenders 21 years old and older because both the Ammiano bill and RCTC proposition would prohibit marijuana use for those under 21. The table provides the estimates in terms of costs in millions of dollars; Table 5.3 shows the percentage those costs represent by component.

There are two main reasons that Miron's earlier and oft-cited estimate (2005) is so much higher than ours or Gieringer's (2009). First, Miron prorates the entire policing budget in proportion to the number of arrests by type (marijuana versus other), but police do many things besides arrest people (e.g., emergency response, traffic control), and not all arrests are equally

Table 5.2
Summary of Estimates of the Costs of Enforcing Marijuana Prohibition in California, Millions of Dollars

Components	Our Estimate (all offenders)	Our Estimate (21+-year-olds)	Gieringer (2009)	Miron (2005)	Miron (2010)
Policing	90–105	59–74	12.4	228.0	412.6
Adjudication	65–80	43–52	84.73	681.8	819.1
Corrections	90–145	88–141	102.9	71.7	659.8
Calif. marijuana eradication program			3.8		
Total	245–330	190–267	203.8	981.5	1,867.2

Table 5.3
Summary of Estimates of the Costs of Enforcing Marijuana Prohibition in California, Percentage per Component

Component	Our Estimate (all offenders)	Our Estimate (21+-year-olds)	Gieringer (2009)	Miron (2005)	Miron (2010)
Policing	~34	~29	6	23	22
Adjudication	~25	~21	42	69	44
Corrections	~41	~50	50	7	35
Calif. marijuana eradication program			2		
Revenues from fines and seizures			−1		

expensive (Aos et al., 2001, 2006). Marijuana arrests are mostly misdemeanors and so are not as expensive, on average, as other types of arrests.[2] Gieringer's (2009) $12.4 million figure for policing is lower because he assumes that misdemeanor arrest costs are completely offset by collection of fines; we are skeptical because fines often cost as much to collect as they are worth (Piehl and Williams, 2010).

Second, Miron's (2005) adjudication and Miron's (2010) adjudication and incarceration costs are much larger than Gieringer's or our estimates because Miron prorates all drug-related prosecution and incarceration costs across drugs in proportion to the fraction of sales and manufacturing arrests by drug. However, marijuana offenders are less likely to be prosecuted than other drug offenders, and they receive shorter sentences if they are prosecuted (see analysis in Caulkins, 2010a). Thus, such prorating assigns far too much of drug-related incarceration costs to marijuana.

---

[2] We combine information about the number of marijuana cases in which a complaint was sought with Aos et al.'s (2001, 2006) figures for the unit cost per conviction for drug offenses and misdemeanors to estimate adjudication costs for marijuana enforcement of $65 million to $80 million. These could be slight underestimates inasmuch as there are more complaints than convictions; so, dividing court costs across convictions, not complaints, ought to generate a slightly higher figure. However, the Aos et al.–derived cost parameters are substantially higher than Albert-Goldberg's (2009) estimates based on Los Angeles County information.

There are many limitations to our estimate's precision and completeness. However, those limitations largely apply to the previous estimates. To the extent that participants in the debate about marijuana legalization in California want to use estimates of this sort, we believe that the figures provided here are more defensible than those that assume that the annual criminal-justice costs are greater than or equal to $1 billion.

A distinct question is whether the California state budget savings from marijuana legalization would equal the current amount now being spent on marijuana prohibition. It likely would not for at least three reasons: (1) Freed resources may be used for other purposes rather than refunded to the taxpayer; (2) most of the criminal-justice resources associated with marijuana enforcement involve local and county, not state, agencies; and (3) there would be new administrative, regulatory, and even enforcement costs of managing the legalized distribution of marijuana.

Treatment Costs

In 2009, there were more than 32,000 treatment admissions in California with marijuana listed as the primary drug of abuse (HHS, 2009). A principal concern of legalization opponents is that, if marijuana consumption rises, dependence will rise and place a further burden on drug treatment systems. However, in California (as in many states), a large share (52 percent in 2009) of drug treatment admissions comes through criminal-justice referrals. Presumably, if marijuana is legalized, fewer people would be transferred to treatment by the criminal-justice system.[3] Such a reduction might pertain only to adults, because youth possession would still be illegal. And, in the case of California, those under the age of 21 represent 62 percent of all the marijuana primary treatment episodes (SAMHSA, undated).

We are unaware of studies that examine how dependence, particularly among youth, changes in response to a change in prices or legalization. Thus, it is difficult to estimate how dependence and related treatment costs will change. Nonetheless, it is worth considering what would happen if (1) non–criminal-justice referrals to marijuana treatment for adults occur in the same proportion to total consumption as they do today, (2) criminal-justice referrals of youths occur at a rate that is similar to what we currently observe, (3) the number of people seeking treatment for abuse or dependence is proportional to the number of regular users, and (4) prices decline by 75 percent.[4] Of course, there are numerous reasons that these assumptions might overestimate or underestimate what will happen to the number of people seeking treatment, but these assumptions are not unreasonable. They imply an extra 2,544 treatment admissions per year.

At a weighted average price of marijuana treatment of $575 (Pacula, 2010a), this would result in a $1.5 million increase in total spending on treatment, of which perhaps $1 million would fall on the taxpayer. We tested the sensitivity of this finding to alternative assumptions (e.g., regarding the fraction of current criminal-justice adult cases that might end up in treatment even with a policy change). The costs to taxpayers could be larger, perhaps even six

---

[3]   Referrals to treatment with marijuana as the primary drug of abuse might occur for other reasons, such as driving while intoxicated, and it is not possible to determine the extent to which this is the case. From a public-health standpoint, a reduction in criminal-justice diversions to treatment might mean an increase in unmet need for treatment, which itself could have other impacts on Californians and on state expenditures. It is possible that these averted cases will find their way to treatment through other paths.

[4]   The interested reader is encouraged to read Pacula (2010a) for more-explicit details and sensitivity analyses.

times larger, but that would still total only a few million dollars, whereas other outcomes are denominated in the tens or hundreds of millions of dollars. Hence, it is unlikely that increased treatment costs will have much of an impact on the bottom line in terms of net budgetary cost of marijuana legalization.

Other Health Costs

The chemical properties and method of administration of marijuana make serious, acute health problems rare when used in moderation or even in excess. However, as an empirical matter, marijuana use does cause health outcomes that lead users to seek immediate medical attention through emergency departments (EDs) and hospitals. These are a particularly costly form of health care, so it is worth considering whether a legalization-induced increase in ED episodes or other hospitalizations would have significant budgetary effects.[5]

In his examination of time-series data, Grossman (2005) finds that a 10-percent decline in the price of marijuana would be associated with an increase in marijuana-involved ED episodes of between 2.65 percent and 11.9 percent. We use this finding to predict what might happen to ED episodes in California given our best estimates of what the probable change in price would be with legalization. To do so, we must start with assumptions about the baseline rates of marijuana-involved ED visits involving only marijuana for the state of California,[6] assumptions about the fraction of these visits that can be causally attributed to marijuana (varied, but started at 20 percent), and information on the fraction of ED visits paid for by the taxpayers (60 percent).[7] The hypothesized change in these adjusted baseline ED rates caused by an increase in consumption due to a 75-percent reduction in the price and a 35-percent increase from nonprice factors is a rise in ED rates between 29 percent and 130 percent. This translates into a cost of marijuana-involved ED episodes to taxpayers in the range of $1.9 million to $2.6 million, small despite episodes in the thousands due to the relatively low presumed average cost per ED visit ($614). Even if we assume that 90 percent of all episodes are causally from marijuana, the ultimate cost to taxpayers is on the order of tens of millions of dollars, which is relatively small compared to estimates of criminal-justice expenditures or potential tax revenue.

There are also costs related to people admitted into the hospital beyond what is captured in the cost of the ED visits. Throughout California in 2008, there were 181 admissions to hospitals in which marijuana abuse or dependence was listed as the primary reason for the hospitalization. Even though the average charge per episode exceeded $22,000, the total cost of these episodes is just over $2 million, so relatively small vis-à-vis the other costs and savings. Perhaps more important from a cost perspective are the additional 25,000 admissions

---

[5] It is possible that legalization will lead to more marijuana being consumed bundled with other products (e.g., beer, brownies), so mode of administration might shift somewhat toward modes that make it more difficult for users to titrate their dose.

[6] As rates are not available for the entire state, we use available data from two California cities (San Diego and San Francisco) that are part of the Drug Abuse Warning Network. Our rates per 100,000 residents are 68.9 (low, from San Diego) and 92 (from San Francisco). Assuming that the rate for the entire state falls within this range, the rates for these two cities are used as bounds for the baseline and adjusted for alternative assumptions regarding the fraction of these episodes that are causally attributable to marijuana.

[7] Details of these calculations are in Pacula (2010a).

for which marijuana is listed as a supplemental diagnosis (second, third, or fourth diagnosis).[8] Of these cases, nearly 4,000 were for schizophrenia (with an average charge of $20,300 per episode) and another 2,300 were for psychoses (with an average cost of $12,700). As the scientific literature is still unclear as to whether marijuana use causes these conditions or just complicates treating them, we do not consider the cost here of these nonprimary diagnoses. More research is needed before an accurate assessment can be conducted, but the implications of these research findings could be important in terms of the burden imposed. For more details on this, see Pacula (2010a).

Regulation Costs

If marijuana is legalized and taxed like alcohol or tobacco, this will create a host of questions for state and local governments. For example, governments will have to decide on the tax rate, licensing regime, optimal number of licenses, and how age restrictions will be enforced. The costs and revenues associated with legalization will depend both on the type of regulations established and the effort put into enforcing them.

There are many options for regulating marijuana, and one need look no further than alcohol regulation for ideas about different approaches. For example, in some states (e.g., Pennsylvania, Utah), liquor can be sold only in state-run stores with limited hours, while, in other states, liquor can be sold in gas stations (e.g., Missouri, Wisconsin). Also, marijuana's physical properties (marijuana is very low in weight and low in volume per unit value) open up a range of alternative regulatory systems (e.g., mail order).

It is important to note that the cost of regulation is a choice variable, not an outcome variable. If the RCTC proposition passes, each local government will be able to determine the number of producers and retail outlets within its jurisdiction. While we do not know how many outlets there could be, it may be possible to gain some insight into this by looking at the number of outlets selling tobacco, alcohol, and other goods in California (Table 5.4).

Nearly 15 million Californians are current alcohol users (i.e., they reported using in the past month). If there is a regulatory environment that allows the same licensee-to–current user ratio for marijuana, and we assume, for this calculation, that legalization will double the number of current marijuana users, then there would be on the order of 8,000 off-site marijuana licensees. But this may not be the best way to think about the number of outlets.[9] If marijuana were sold wherever tobacco was sold in California, there would be close to 38,000 outlets. Alternatively, if a decision were made to allow only existing medical-marijuana dispensaries to distribute legal marijuana, the number of outlets might be on the order of 1,000.

There could be just as much variation in the per-outlet regulation costs. For example, the California ABC, which is tasked with regulating alcohol suppliers throughout the state, has an annual budget of $52 million. Dividing this by the total number of alcohol outlets (on- and off-site; ABC, 2009) would put the average cost per outlet at approximately $650. Since some of the regulation costs come from sanctioning and shutting down problem suppliers, this $650, which is based on the number of existing licensees, may be inflated. This calculation also assumes that the regulation costs are generally the same for on- and off-site premises. Also, this

---

[8] Author's own calculation using 2008 California Office of Statewide Health Planning and Development (OSHPD) data, identifying a primary marijuana admission as one in which the primary diagnosis code was either 304.3X or 305.2X.

[9] 30,000 off-site licensees ÷ 15 million current alcohol users × 4 million current marijuana users post-legalization = 8,000 off-site licensees.

Table 5.4
Number of Retail Outlets for Selling Various Products in California

Type of Outlet	Number (Year)	Source
Medical-marijuana dispensaries and delivery services	>750 (May 2010)	Our estimate[a]
Pharmacies selling tobacco in California	>3,000 (2003)	County of Los Angeles Breath (2006)
Gasoline stations with convenience stores	~6,000 (2007)	Census (2009)
Off-site alcohol licensees	~30,000 (2009)	ABC (2009)
Tobacco retailers	~38,000 (2009)	BOE (2009a)

[a] We are not aware of estimates of the total number of medical-marijuana outlets in California, but we guess that, as of May 2010, the number probably exceeds 750. While there were reports of there being 1,000 dispensaries in Los Angeles alone, this was an overestimate. The real number is closer to 500–600 (Hoeffel, 2010), and, in June 2010, the city is starting the process of shutting down the majority. As for other jurisdictions, the city of San Jose estimates that it has 60 dispensaries ("San Jose City Council Discusses Pot Dispensary Regulation," 2010), and, in Santa Barbara, some report approximately 20 dispensaries (Canelon, 2009). The number of dispensaries in San Francisco has been the subject of debate, with federal officials putting the figure above 60 and local officials putting the figure closer to 25 (Coté et al., 2008). Hoeffel (2009b) reports that, in December 2009, Oakland had four dispensaries, Berkeley three, Palm Springs two, West Hollywood four, and Sebastopol two. While this is not a comprehensive list, it is informative. The National Organization for the Reform of Marijuana Laws (NORML) office in California lists more than 500 dispensaries on its website for the state (about 100–150 are in the Los Angeles–Long Beach area), but it does not claim that this list is comprehensive or up-to-date (California NORML, undated). There are also delivery services that are not necessarily linked with storefront dispensaries. As of May 2010, we are reasonably confident that the number of outlets selling medical marijuana exceeded 750 and would not be surprised if the true number were closer to 1,000.

estimate may be low, because there are other expenditures associated with supply-side regulation. But even if the true figure were ten times this amount, it would still be lower than the $19,000 reportedly required per dispensary for the Los Angeles Police Department (LAPD) to inspect and audit medical-marijuana dispensaries in Los Angeles.[10]

We are uncomfortable projecting the regulatory costs associated with legalizing marijuana supply, but we want to highlight that the number could range dramatically depending on the number of suppliers and the intensity of enforcement.[11] ABC is funded through license fees, and this is the regime proposed in the Ammiano bill. In this case, suppliers would cover

---

[10] There has been a tremendous debate in Los Angeles about the appropriate number of medical-marijuana dispensaries in the city. During reform debate, there was discussion about limiting the number of dispensaries to 70 and creating a separate inspection and audit unit within LAPD. Los Angeles Police Commander Patrick M. Gannon "estimated that a 14-employee team would be needed to watch 70 dispensaries and would cost about $1.3 million to operate" (Hoeffel, 2009a). We confirmed with the LAPD that this was an annual figure that would put the regulation cost per dispensary at nearly $19,000.

[11] Another potential regulatory cost could involve inspection and quality control. Dale Gieringer, the director of California NORML, observes that marijuana potency and contamination testing can be done for $100 per sample (Gieringer, 2010). The cost burden of such testing and inspection depends on how large a sample can be tested at once. If every ounce has to be tested individually, the cost burden at Gieringer's suggested rate would obviously be $100 per ounce. If a house-based operation producing 546 pounds per year in four equal-size harvests could somehow have an entire quarter's harvest tested at once, the cost would fall below $0.05 per ounce. This is an essentially nihilistic range, so we prefer to think of the estimates here as those that would pertain if inspection and compliance costs were merely akin to those of existing agricultural products, which is to say negligible relative to costs in the hundreds of dollars per pound.

much of the costs associated with regulating supply, thus leading to a small net impact on government expenditures.

Indirect Effects

This section focuses on some nonbudgetary effects of legalization: dependence and abuse, drugged driving, and the use of other substances. While each can have important implications for the budget (some of which are included in the previous section), here we stress some non-budget effects that may be of interest. It is important to note that we do not provide a comprehensive assessment of all potential health outcomes associated with marijuana use (e.g., chronic respiratory effects, psychological effects). For reviews of these literatures, please see Hall and Pacula (2003) and Hall and Degenhardt (2009).

Dependence and Abuse

How would the number of marijuana users meeting clinical criteria for abuse or dependence change with a change in the policy? Over this decade, the number of users meeting these criteria in the previous year as a fraction of people reporting use of marijuana in the past year in nationally representative samples has been fairly stable (~16 percent). One way to project what could happen to dependent users post-legalization is to assume that this relationship between the number dependent and past-year users remains the same.

We start by making an assumption about legalization's effect on consumption. For this example, we consider a 58-percent increase in annual consumption and refer interested readers to Pacula (2010a) for more information about this starting value. With 525,000 users estimated to meet *Diagnostic and Statistical Manual of Mental Disorders*, 4th ed. (DSM-IV) criteria for marijuana abuse or dependence in California in 2009 (Pacula, 2010a), a 58-percent increase would suggest a rise of 305,000, bringing the total number of users meeting clinical criteria for abuse or dependence to 830,000. Of course, there is tremendous uncertainty surrounding this number because of uncertainty about the baseline assumptions that generated the predicted change in annual prevalence. If we adopt alternative plausible assumptions, we generate a range of 144,000 to 380,000, implying that the total number of users meeting clinical criteria for abuse or dependence would be in the range of 669,000 to 905,000.

There are currently no estimates in the literature of the social cost of a user meeting clinical criteria for abuse or dependence; thus, it is not possible to quantify this increase's budgetary impact on California taxpayers. But, to the extent that dependence and abuse impose costs in the form of reduced productivity, higher health-care costs, or lost time with the family, a rise in dependence represents a real loss to the citizens of California.

Drugged Driving

While driving under the influence of marijuana or any other intoxicating substance can be risky, a question remains about whether marijuana use impairs individuals sufficiently to cause crashes and fatalities. While there is significant experimental literature suggesting a diminished effect on response rates and performance under very strictly controlled conditions, evidence from epidemiological studies has been less conclusive (Ramaekers et al., 2004; Blows et al., 2005). The notable exception in the literature are cases in which alcohol is used in conjunction with marijuana, in which case the evidence is clear that the combined effect of these two drugs impairs driving significantly more than alcohol alone (Bramness, Khiabani, and Mørland, 2010; Jones et al., 2003; Dussault et al., 2002). Given the current uncertainty of the science in determining the role of marijuana use alone in accidents, it is impossible to determine how much an increase in marijuana use would translate into more accidents or, worse yet, fatal crashes.

However, a simple calculation suggests that, *if* someone believes that marijuana is causally responsible for many crashes that involve marijuana using drivers, legalization's effect on crashes could be a first-order concern for them. Based on Fatality Analysis Reporting System (FARS) data, Crancer and Crancer (2010) report that blood tests established that one or both drivers had used marijuana near the time of the accident in 5.5 percent of passenger-vehicle fatal crashes (2008 in California). Causality is complicated in multicar crashes, but, even just considering single-vehicle fatal crashes, Crancer and Crancer found that 126 fatalities in crashes with marijuana involved drivers, 75 percent of whom had alcohol levels below 0.08.

There is no empirical evidence concerning an elasticity of fatal accident rates with respect to marijuana price, prevalence, or quantity consumed, and, as we have underscored repeatedly, there is enormous uncertainty concerning how legalization might affect those outcomes. However, 50- or 100-percent increases in use cannot be ruled out; nor can the possibility that marijuana-involved traffic crashes would increase proportionally with use. So it would be hard to dismiss out of hand worries that marijuana legalization could increase traffic fatalities by at least 60 per year (126 × 50% = 63)—especially since this represents increases in fatalities associated only with single-vehicle crashes and ignores the role marijuana might play in multivehicle fatalities. See Pacula (2010a) for a more detailed analysis.

There is no satisfactory way to compare the importance of some number of traffic deaths to dollar-denominated outcomes, such as tax revenues, but, when economists are forced to come up with such a number, they often use figures on the order of $4 million to $9 million per death (Viscusi and Aldy, 2003). Whereas we are reasonably confident that additional costs of marijuana treatment and of ED mentions and hospitalizations related directly to use per se are not first-order concerns, we cannot rule out that possibility with respect to legalization's effects on drugged driving.

Use of Other Substances

Legalization will reduce marijuana prices and increase marijuana use. Either effect could affect the use of other substances. We take them up in reverse order.

Increased marijuana use could lead to greater use of other substances in various ways. For example, it is possible that becoming dependent on marijuana affects neural pathways in a way that increases vulnerability to abusing other substances. However, almost all the literature and controversy concerns a possible causal effect of use short of dependence.

The use of marijuana typically precedes the use of such substances as cocaine and heroin, and people who use marijuana earlier and more heavily are more likely to go on to more and heavier use of these substances (Kandel, 2002). These facts have given rise to the so-called gateway hypothesis—the hypothesis being that the pattern is not merely coincidence but instead reflects causal linkages, so that anything that increases or reduces use of marijuana might thereby cause an increase or reduction in use of these other substances.

Few topics in the drug-policy literature have stirred greater passions than the gateway hypothesis. While everyone agrees about the descriptive facts (e.g., cocaine use is usually preceded by marijuana use), there are sharp differences about whether the patterns reflect a causal relationship and, if so, what the causal mechanism is. Skeptics are fond of pointing out that cocaine use is also usually preceded by drinking milk (i.e., most cocaine users tried milk before they first experimented with cocaine, but no one believes that drinking milk puts one at risk for greater cocaine use).

The gateway effect, if it exists, has at least two potential and quite different sources (Mac-Coun, 1998). One interpretation is that it is an effect of the drug use itself (e.g., trying marijuana increases the taste for other drugs or leads users to believe that other substances are more pleasurable or less risky than previously supposed). A second interpretation stresses peer groups and social interactions. Acquiring and using marijuana regularly may lead to differentially associating with peers who have attitudes and behaviors that are prodrug generally, not only with respect to marijuana. One version of this is the possibility that those peers will include people who sell other drugs, reducing the difficulty of locating potential supplies. If the latter is the explanation, then legalization might reduce the likelihood of moving on to harder drugs compared to the current situation.

Many studies have examined the gateway effect, and Room et al. (2010, p. 35) provide a concise appraisal of the international, multidisciplinary evidence:

> Cannabis use is more strongly associated with other illicit drug use than alcohol or tobacco use, and the earliest and most frequent cannabis users are the most likely to use other illicit drugs. Animal studies provide some biological plausibility for a causal relationship between cannabis and other types of illicit drug use. Well-controlled longitudinal studies suggest that selective recruitment to cannabis use does not wholly explain the association between cannabis use and the use of other illicit drugs. This is supported by discordant twin studies [that] suggest that shared genes and environment do not wholly explain the association. Nonetheless, it has been difficult to exclude the hypothesis that the pattern of use reflects the common characteristics of those who use cannabis and other drugs.

We say nothing more about gateway effects because there simply is no consensus about magnitudes of those effects that would provide a basis for translating our projections of changes in marijuana use into projections of effects on other substances.

In two key respects, the idea of a gateway effect is related to, but conceptually distinct from, the economic concept of cross-price elasticity. Cross-price elasticity helps us think about how a change in the price of good A influences the consumption of good B, and the empirical studies focus on contemporaneous effects. In contrast, gateway effects are thought of in terms of long-run pathways or "careers" of drug use, and they pertain primarily to tastes or preferences, and sometimes availability, rather than price effects.

Price effects can work in either direction. Two goods are considered substitutes for one another if an increase in the price of good A leads to an increase in the demand for good B. They are considered complements to one another if an increase in the price of good A leads to a decrease in the demand for goods A and B. Most of the cross-price literature on marijuana has focused on effects on alcohol, tobacco, and cocaine use. Some of it looks at the effect of reductions in penalties for marijuana use, which can be thought of as a reduction in the total cost (price) of using marijuana (see, e.g., Pacula, 1998a; Williams and Mahmoudi, 2004, for useful reviews of this literature).

Alcohol. Much of this research focuses on the effect of marijuana-decriminalization policies on self-reported alcohol use, and the findings are mixed (e.g., Chaloupka and Laixuthai,

1997; Pacula, 1998a; Saffer and Chaloupka, 1999). This is not surprising, because it is unclear what decriminalization status actually measures (Pacula, Chriqui, and King, 2003; MacCoun et al., 2009). Very few studies examine how changes in the money price of marijuana influences alcohol consumption, and these studies either produce inconsistent results (Chaloupka and Laixuthai, 1997)[12] or find that the effect is close to 0 (Williams et al., 2004).[13] The latter study focuses only on the effect of changes in marijuana prices on the probability of being a past-month alcohol user for college students. This highlights two important caveats. First, there is a difference between participation and total quantity demanded. Even if the changes in marijuana prices did not influence the probability of alcohol consumption, they may well have influenced the amount consumed by those who decided to use. Second, we should be careful about extrapolating the results from one group (in this case, college students) to the rest of the population.

Tobacco. There are a few studies suggesting that increases in tobacco taxes (which reduce tobacco use) lead to decreases in marijuana prevalence (Pacula, 1998a, 1998b; Chaloupka, Grossman, and Tauras, 1999). However, we must be cautious, because we cannot necessarily assume a reciprocal relationship. We are unaware of any studies of tobacco demand that include the money price of marijuana. However, Farrelly et al. (2001) use a proxy for marijuana use, and their results suggest that, when marijuana use goes up, so does tobacco use.[14]

Cocaine. A number of studies suggest that marijuana and cocaine are economic complements, but many of these studies use the problematic decriminalization variable as a proxy for marijuana price (Thies and Register, 1993; Grossman and Chaloupka, 1998; Saffer and Chaloupka, 1999). Williams and colleagues (2006) use actual marijuana prices in their analysis of cocaine use among college students in the United States. For college students in the 1990s, they estimate the cross-price participation elasticity for cocaine to be between –0.44 and –0.49. This means that a 10-percent decrease in the price of marijuana would increase the prevalence of cocaine use by 4.4 to 4.9 percent.[15]

While the debate about marijuana use's effect on the use of other substances is far from settled, it is critical to note that the existing research has generally focused on how marginal changes in prices or fines influence consumption of other substances. This literature does not examine what happens after a large shock. Since marijuana legalization would likely be more

---

[12] The authors argue that more weight should be given to the commercial-grade findings (which suggest that marijuana and alcohol are substitutes) because there was a lot of measurement error with sinsemilla and youth are more likely to use commercial grade since it is cheaper.

[13] Williams et al. (2004) found a statistically significant negative marijuana price effect on 30-day alcohol use ($z = -2.03$), thus suggesting that marijuana and alcohol are complementary goods. However, this effect is very small. The marginal effect of -0.0009 suggests that, ceteris paribus, a $10 increase in the price of an ounce of commercial-grade marijuana (which would represent a 16-percent increase in the mean price; 1999 dollars) decreases the probability that a college student uses alcohol in the previous month by 0.009 percentage points. With 69 percent of the respondents reporting past-month alcohol use, this equates to a 0.013-percent decrease in prevalence. The effect on quantity of alcohol consumed was not measured.

[14] The proxy is the marijuana price by dividing the number of juvenile arrests for marijuana by the number of marijuana users aged 12–20 for each state-year. The authors also include information about marijuana fines and report that the results were consistent with a complementary relationship but were not statistically significant.

[15] The authors also estimated the cross-price participation elasticity for marijuana, and the results confirmed the complementary relationship and were consistent with another study (DeSimone and Farrelly, 2003).

than a marginal change (in terms of price, stigma, criminal risk, and, possibly, availability), it is unclear how these results based on smaller changes would extrapolate.

CHAPTER SIX

Considering Alternative Scenarios

Many assumptions are embedded in the structure of our model. In this chapter, we consider alternative assumptions, focusing on those we think could have important impacts or have received attention in the debate about the Ammiano bill or the RCTC proposition. We stress that this is not an exhaustive list of scenarios.

A Federal Response

We cannot overstate the importance of the potential federal response. Legalizing marijuana production would bring California law into direct conflict with federal law, as well as with various international treaties that the United States has signed pertaining to drug control. A potential federal response would be to allocate more federal law-enforcement resources to prosecuting people in California for violating federal marijuana laws. Another potential response would be for the federal government to launch a lawsuit against the State of California. It is possible that the interstate-commerce clause gives clear supremacy to federal law, but it is not inconceivable that a test case stemming from marijuana legalization might provoke new rulings concerning federalism.[1]

Even without a full-blown constitutional crisis, California legalization probably would not play well in Congress. Another response would be to withhold federal appropriations. When the federal government wanted to "strong-arm" reluctant states into increasing the drinking age, it passed the Uniform Minimum Drinking Age Act of 1984 (Pub. L. 98-363), which withheld 10 percent of federal highway dollars from states that did not make it illegal for those under 21 to purchase or publicly possess alcohol.[2] If Congress withheld 10 percent of federal highway dollars from California (i.e., 10 percent × $3 billion), that could, for example, offset the potential criminal justice "savings" (California Department of Transportation,

---

[1] The Obama administration has clearly sought to minimize conflict around the production of marijuana for medical purposes, but it has not yet had to establish a position on production for recreational use. Even without a Supreme Court ruling, a new administration could decide to reverse this stance and enforce federal laws against activity California has legalized, provoking a test case, which would unquestionably be violated by commercial cultivation and sale. Related to this, Mikos (2009) contends that state marijuana laws "have not been, and, more interestingly, cannot be preempted by Congress, given constraints imposed on Congress's preemption power by the anti-commandeering rule, properly understood."

[2] According to Title 23 of the U.S. Code,

> The Secretary shall withhold 10 per centum of the amount required to be apportioned to any State under each of sections 104 (b)(1), 104 (b)(3), and 104 (b)(4) [all transportation statutes] of this title on the first day of each fiscal year after the second fiscal year beginning after September 30, 1985, in which the purchase or public possession in such State of any alcoholic beverage by a person who is less than twenty-one years of age is lawful. (23 U.S.C. §158)

undated). Cooley (2010) raises the possibility that the RCTC proposition would make California noncompliant with the Anti–Drug Abuse Act of 1988 (Pub. L. 100-690); we make no judgments about whether Cooley is right, but we note that, if he were, that could have even greater consequences.[3]

If the federal threat is serious enough, it could essentially eliminate legal sales and, thus, the possibility of generating any tax revenue. But, at the other extreme, if the federal government does not get involved, California could generate an even larger amount of revenue by exporting sinsemilla to other states (a possibility that is discussed in the next section). An intermediate possibility would be a strong federal response against trafficking and production but a more muted response at the retail and consumer levels, which might produce a Dutch-style partial-legalization regime. Related to this, if the RCTC proposition passes and decision-makers are worried about a "race to the bottom" with respect to taxes (which is discussed in more detail later in this chapter), one option would be for federal officials to use their considerable enforcement discretion to tolerate production in jurisdictions that kept the tax rate above a certain threshold.[4] Of course, these are not the only options available to the federal government.

Taxing Exports to Other States

The results discussed thus far have focused on what would happen to consumption in California and the tax revenues deriving from that consumption. While we do not know how much marijuana California currently exports to other states, such activity would likely increase post-legalization, given the expected drops in California production and processing costs. Indeed, as Bond and Caulkins (2010) note, sinsemilla produced legally in California would undercut sinsemilla prices throughout almost the entire United States, even if it is successfully taxed at $50 per ounce and allowance is made for the cost of smuggling illegal marijuana. Hence, legalizing marijuana in California could depress sinsemilla prices and increase consumption throughout the nation. Furthermore, if the marijuana smuggled out of California were diverted from the legal distribution system after taxes had been collected, then California would collect tax revenues on those exports. Since the rest of the lower 48 states have about six times as many marijuana users as does California, taxes on exports could dramatically increase California's tax revenues. Some such tax revenues are almost certain, even if only from "drug tourists" traveling from other states to buy personal consumption amounts (as happens in the Netherlands). However, unless purchase-quantity limits are enforced, it could also happen on a commercial scale.

The numbers behind this scenario are straightforward. A legal, taxed price of $91 per ounce is equivalent to $1,450 per pound. The price gradient observed today for marijuana is about $450 per pound per thousand miles one moves away from its source (e.g., away from Mexico for commercial-grade marijuana; Bond and Caulkins, 2010). So, for example,

---

[3]   Specifically, Cooley notes that the drug-testing provision in the RCTC proposition is in conflict with "The Federal Drug-Free Workplace Act of 1988 [which] requires that all employers who receive government grants and contracts greater than $100,000 maintain a drug-free workplace."

[4]   The federal government could also use this approach to encourage other restrictions on production, advertising, potency, an so on.

the cost of smuggling the 2,500 miles from San Francisco to Washington, D.C., is about 2.5 × $450 = $1,125 per pound. Adding that to the purchase price gives a total cost ($2,575 per pound), that is considerably below the current wholesale price of sinsemilla in the Maryland/ Virginia area (roughly $4,000 per pound). The California-grown sinsemilla would be even more competitive if it were purchased at post-legalization wholesale prices (closer to $1,250 per pound, including all taxes).

The economics are different for commercial-grade marijuana. Legal commercial-grade marijuana from California taxed at $50 per ounce ($800 per pound) would not be cost-competitive with commercial-grade from Mexico, which sells within the United States along the southwest border for $300–$600 per pound. If California (and the federal enforcement agencies) allowed farm-based cultivation and tax rates were lower, the situation would be different because mechanized farming can produce marijuana for well below $300–$600 per pound; however, it seems unlikely that federal agencies would allow such brazen production.

Competition between California sinsemilla and Mexican commercial-grade would be tighter on a price-per-unit-of-THC basis. With a lower tax (e.g., $5 per ounce), California-grown sinsemilla would win almost everywhere; with a higher tax (e.g., $50 per ounce), the winner would vary by location, because the same smuggling cost per pound generates a lower smuggling cost per unit of THC for sinsemilla than for commercial grade.

Thus, when it comes to California's tax revenue from exports, much depends on particulars about the tax rate and whether the marijuana would be diverted at the wholesale or retail level and before or after taxes are collected. However, even if California merely captured the bulk of the sinsemilla market with taxed exports, California tax revenues could substantially increase. (In round terms, there are six times as many marijuana users outside of California as in California, and sinsemilla probably accounts for close to one-tenth of the total quantity consumed nationally.[5]) A tripling or even quadrupling of tax revenues is not implausible under the right circumstances.

Trying to Use the Excise Tax to Keep Prices at the Current Level

For most of our analyses, we have focused on the $50-per-ounce excise tax, because that is the level listed in the Ammiano bill and it receives the most attention in the debate in California. As we noted earlier, the RCTC proposition allows each local jurisdiction to determine the tax rate. Given the large increase in use expected to come with a large decrease in production costs and distribution costs, one possibility would be to use the excise tax to offset the cost reduction.

The excise tax required to keep prices at their current levels would be high. The current price for an ounce of sinsemilla is close to $375, and we expect the pretax price to fall to $38 per ounce, which accounts for production, markups, and distribution. This would suggest that the minimum excise tax that would be sufficient to guarantee no drop in retail prices would be $337 per ounce, or roughly a 700-percent tax.[6] Table 3.1 in Chapter Three shows that the

---

[5]   It is impossible to know what this number is with certainty. We generated this figure based on data from the National Institute on Drug Abuse (2008), Gieringer (1994), and our own analyses of marijuana purchase questions in the Arrestee Drug Abuse Monitoring Program (ADAM) and NSDUH.

[6]   This would likely be a minimum, because a tax that high would likely induce a shift toward forms of marijuana with greater THC content. The average THC content of Nederwiet is roughly double that of sinsemilla in the United States. The

typical tax per gram for cigarettes is \$0.02 and that, for marijuana with the \$50-per-ounce tax, it would be \$1.76. With a \$337 tax per ounce, the tax per gram would increase to \$11.89 per gram. While this situation would be ripe for tax evasion, evasion is a function of the expected sanction faced by those selling and purchasing the untaxed marijuana. The level, and credibility, of this enforcement threat is a choice variable. Whether the tax receipts could more than offset the costs associated with the increase in enforcement against the gray market is an empirical question.[7]

The legalization of home production could also affect the ability to use taxes to offset the anticipated price drop. The number of marijuana users who report on surveys that they grow their own is in the few hundreds of thousands (Caulkins and Pacula, 2006), and this might become more common after it is legalized. As noted earlier, the allowed 5-foot–by–5-foot growing area under the RCTC proposition is sufficient to supply quite a few typical users.

One Jurisdiction "Defecting" from an Otherwise High Tax Rate

The Ammiano bill would impose a uniform \$50-per-ounce tax rate (at least unless the resulting revenues exceeded spending on drug prevention), but the RCTC proposition would delegate tax rate setting to the 478 individual cities and 58 counties. So far, we have assumed that the tax rate would be uniform throughout the state, but that does not seem likely under the RCTC proposition. To see why, consider the following thought experiment.

Suppose for the sake of argument that initially all consumption were supplied from jurisdictions imposing a \$50-per-ounce tax, and imagine a single jurisdiction that is generally favorable toward the marijuana industry. Suppose that it is a single county with 2 percent of California's population. Initially, that county would be collecting essentially 2 percent of the tax revenues. Supposing that tax evasion were initially 50 percent, the county would collect about \$10 million out of the \$520 million tax total.[8]

However, if the county were clever, it might cut its excise tax rate, say, to \$5 per ounce. That would mean that marijuana purchased within its borders would cost only \$46 per ounce, whereas, everywhere else, it would remain at \$91 per ounce. A \$45-per-ounce difference (\$720 per pound) would probably be enough to capture sales from much of the rest of the state; at \$46 per ounce, the legal price in this county would even undercut the originally assumed gray-market price of \$68 per ounce being paid by the 50 percent of the market that was evading taxes.

Collecting \$5 per ounce (as well as sales tax) on much of the state's consumption would be more lucrative than collecting \$50 per ounce on 2 percent of the 50 percent of consumption that had previously been successfully taxed, particularly because lowering the effective

---

tax per ounce on Nederwiet-quality marijuana necessary to preserve the current cost per unit of THC would be closer to \$600 per ounce.

[7] It is worth nothing, though, that the profit per unit weight made by evading such a tax would be as large as the profit per unit weight of smuggling cocaine across the border into the United States, something we have failed to completely deter despite significant effort and sanctions (Caulkins and Reuter, 2010).

[8] The county gets slightly less than 2 percent of the tax revenues because the state portion of sales tax would go to Sacramento; the county would get 2 percent of the rest.

price to consumers would increase consumption.[9] Note that this competition for tax revenues would not only be over sales to California consumers but also over legal sales to people who would then illegally smuggle the marijuana to other states. Some local consumers might wish to exercise some kind of loyalty by paying taxes to their own county, but consumers in Ohio, for example, would have no such preferences among California jurisdictions; they would want their dealers to buy in whichever California jurisdiction was offering the lowest prices.

Furthermore, if the lower taxes induced more of the production to shift into a county, then the county might get an economic development boost. The average economic development impact of legal marijuana production for the state may not be large, but, concentrated in a single county with 2 percent of the state's population, it would be proportionately more important.

And there are good reasons to suspect that this new tax structure with one county reaping most of the budgetary benefits would be unsustainable. Presumably, other counties that wished to keep their "fair share" of production, sales, and associated tax revenues would match or beat the first county's move. This might precipitate a "race to the bottom" in terms of tax rates, or at least a race down to the point at which tax rate differences no longer swamped other considerations.[10]

The particular numbers just discussed are meant only to illustrate a general point. Unless there is some statewide control of tax rates, it might be difficult to sustain excise taxes at the level contemplated by the Ammiano bill, not only with respect to the risk of tax evasion but also with respect to competition among different local jurisdictions to capture market share by lowering their excise tax rates.

Raising Prices Through Regulation

Recall that we assume that the current price of sinsemilla is $375 per ounce and that this will drop with our baseline parameters to $91 per ounce in a legalized regime, accounting for taxes and retailing costs. One factor that might soften the price decline would be highly burdensome regulatory, testing, inspection, and reporting requirements. To explore this, we consider what would happen if regulatory burden quintupled the wholesale price of marijuana from $26 per ounce to $130 per ounce, driving up the gray-market and legal, taxed prices to $181 and $241 per ounce, respectively (versus $68 and $91 in the base case).

Table 6.1 shows the results, assuming a 25-percent tax evasion (to make it consistent with the base-case scenario). Naturally, consumption is lower, strikingly so with a constant-elasticity-of-demand curve because the nonlinearity in that demand curve becomes most important when prices fall sharply. Just for reference, we also include the BOE estimates for the Ammiano bill, which assumes a $50 excise tax per ounce with no evasion.

---

[9] The precise amounts depend on particular assumptions, but, if, after the tax cut, the county captured 50 percent of state consumption, 25 percent remained at $91 per ounce, and 25 percent remained at the gray-market price of $68, then the county's sales and excise tax revenues would increase sixfold.

[10] If one county's production costs were 20 percent lower than another's (e.g., because of lower electricity rates), that would be the equivalent of a roughly $5-per-ounce advantage; thus, that county could preserve tax rates that were a few dollars per ounce higher than its competitors' rates.

Table 6.1
Projection of Consequences of a Quintupling of Production Costs Relative to the Post-Legalization Baseline ($50-per-ounce excise tax and 25-percent tax evasion)

Cases	Consumption Increase (%)	Tax ($ millions)		
		Excise	Sales	Total
Base case, linear demand	77	602	72	674
Base case, constant-elasticity demand	158	879	105	984
Multiplied wholesale price, linear demand	57	533	297	829
Multiplied wholesale price, constant-elasticity demand	67	567	316	883
BOE analysis of the Ammiano bill (assumes no evasion)	25[a]	990	392	1,382

[a] BOE (2009b) assumes a 50% decrease in price that would increase consumption by 40%, and the $50-per-ounce excise tax would subsequently reduce use by 11%; (1 + 40%) × (1 − 11%) gives a 25% increase in consumption.

The results with respect to tax revenues are quite interesting, albeit heavily dependent on our simple assumption that retailers always mark up by a fixed 33 percent.[11] With that assumption, quintupling the wholesale price effectively quintuples the pretax price and, hence, sales tax revenue per unit sold. Although the higher prices depress consumption and, hence, excise tax revenue, sales tax revenues are three to four times higher. With a constant-elasticity demand curve, that substantially offsets lost excise tax revenue, so total tax revenue falls only 10 percent, even though consumption drops by more than one-third. With linear demand, the extra costs have only a modest effect on consumption (11-percent decline); as a result, total tax revenues actually go up (by 23 percent).

Hence, if the correct model were linear demand, even a completely wasteful regulatory burden (from an economic-efficiency perspective) might increase tax revenues and moderate the increase in consumption (and, thus, the consumption-related consequences discussed in Chapter Five).

Considering Alternative Assumptions About the Slope of the Marijuana Supply Curve

The model presented in this paper assumes that none of the resources employed in legal marijuana production is unduly constrained, so that increased production would not drive up the average cost of production. The technical name for this assumption is a *perfectly elastic supply curve*. Many economists make this simplifying assumption in diverse applications, arguing that, in the long run, it is easy for suppliers to respond to changes in demand. Past efforts to model illegal drug supply have also typically made this assumption (e.g., Reuter and Kleiman, 1986; Rydell and Everingham, 1994; Caulkins et al., 1997; Rhodes et al., 2000). However, it

---

[11] Or, equivalently, that the regulatory burden quintuples costs for retailers as well as producers.

is plausible that the long-run supply curve is not a horizontal line. If the supply curve actually slopes upward, when demand shifts up as a result of the nonprice effects of legalization, prices would increase and thus make the resulting increase in consumption smaller. In particular, the base-case assumption is for a 35-percent increase in demand after legalization. With a constant elasticity of supply, that translates to a 35-percent increase in consumption. With an upward-sloping supply curve, the increase would be smaller. How much smaller depends on the supply elasticity.

We note that there are studies of varying quality suggesting that the long-run supply elasticity of agricultural products is not infinitely elastic and that, in some cases, it is surprisingly small (e.g., Askari and Cummings, 1977; Hertel, 2002). Our simple model already accounts for a tremendous amount of uncertainty, and we chose not to add more complexity by considering multiple supply curves. If one believes that, in the long run, it will not be easy for suppliers to respond to changes in demand, then it may be the case that our model overstates the effect of legalization.

Wildcards

Thus far, this chapter has discussed alternative scenarios that highlight some of the structural uncertainty associated with projecting the effects of marijuana legalization. In this section, we list some other factors and possibilities that show that our parameter variation and scenarios have not exhausted the range of possible outcomes.

Attitudes and Behavior

We included attitudes in our discussion of nonprice effects. It is easiest to think of ways in which legalization might create a more permissive atmosphere that would encourage marijuana use. But attitudes may have more-nuanced and complex effects. For example, Tyler (e.g., Tyler and Huo, 2002) has shown that perceptions of unfairness harm the perceived legitimacy of the police and the courts, especially among racial and ethnic minorities, and that this reduces people's willingness to comply with legal authorities. As another example, Dutch officials often argue that they have deglamorized cannabis by tolerating it (see MacCoun, 1993, for evidence for a forbidden-fruit effect). Thus, some attitudinal effects could have positive social effects. A more pernicious example would be if stereotypes of California would take a sufficiently extreme turn for the worse to result in a loss of business for the state (e.g., in corporate location decisions).

Tourism

California is a major tourist destination. Marijuana legalization would likely be a high-profile action, noted by people around the United States and even abroad. Plausibly, it could influence decisions to vacation in California, positively for some people and negatively for others. We did not explore this issue ourselves but note that tourism in California is an $87.7 billion–per-year industry that generated $5.4 billion in state and local taxes in 2009 (Dean Runyan Associates, 2010); thus, if marijuana legalization hypothetically led to a 10-percent change in tourism,[12]

---

[12] We do not have a particular justification for this 10-percent figure; it is for illustrative purposes only. Coincidentally, it does appear to be consistent with anecdotal evidence from Amsterdam:

the tax effects of that would be of comparable importance to some of the tax revenue projections stemming directly from legalization.

Shifting Food Product Industry to California

Marijuana can be consumed in many ways other than by smoking; for example, it can be added to food (e.g., brownies) and beverages (e.g., beer). This is what we discussed earlier as bundling. It is plausible that marijuana-impregnated products could become an important niche market, but they could only be produced inside California. If currently that product is produced primarily or exclusively outside of California, then this might induce relocation of some production into California, bringing jobs and tax revenues as well. If the producers wish to have only one facility making both marijuana-impregnated and standard products, the requirement that the former be produced in California might even pull some of the standard production into California from other states.

Cross-Price Effects

In Chapter Five, we highlighted the literature examining marijuana use's effect on the use of other substances. While this debate is far from settled, it is important to think about how changes in marijuana use could influence costs through changes in the use of other substances. There is a wide range of outcomes for which aggregate costs or other effects associated with alcohol, tobacco, and so-called hard drugs are five to 15 times greater than those associated with marijuana (Caulkins et al., 2002). Thus, even small cross-price elasticities would imply indirect effects—mediated through changes in consumption of other substances—that could trump the importance of direct effects through changes in marijuana consumption (Kleiman, 1992).

Some specific numbers help make the point. Harwood (2000) estimated the economic cost of alcohol abuse in the United States to be $185 billion in 1998. Adjusting for inflation and prorating by California's share of the U.S. population would suggest economic costs of alcohol abuse in California of about $30 billion. If the cross-price elasticity of alcohol consumption with respect to marijuana prices were as large as 0.1, in absolute value, then a 75-percent reduction in marijuana prices could affect alcohol-related costs in California by $30 billion × 0.1 × 0.75 = $2.25 billion. That is larger than most of the marijuana-specific outcomes we have discussed. We are intentionally vague about the direction of the effect as it could be in either direction, depending on whether marijuana and alcohol (and other substances) are net complements or substitutes after legalization.

A 2007 report by Amsterdam's Department for Research and Statistics shows that of the 4.5 million tourists who spend the night in Amsterdam during a given year, 26 percent visit a coffeeshop. According to the Amsterdam Tourism & Convention Board, 10 percent of tourists even mention this as a primary reason to visit the city. (Amsterdam Tourist Information, 2008)

CHAPTER SEVEN

Concluding Comments

The current California proposals to legalize marijuana would go well beyond cannabis reforms in any other nation to date—even the Dutch cannabis coffee-shop system. California voters and legislators face considerable uncertainty because it is very difficult to estimate how much more marijuana will be consumed in the state or how the change will affect tax revenues, criminal-justice costs, and health-care costs. Nonetheless, we believe that bringing together relevant data in a systematic fashion and developing a model has provided some important insights:

- The pretax retail price of marijuana will substantially decline, likely by more than 80 percent. The price consumers face will depend heavily on taxes, the structure of the regulatory regime, and how taxes and regulations are enforced.
- Consumption will increase, but it is unclear how much because we know neither the shape of the demand curve nor the level of tax evasion (which reduces revenues and the prices that consumers face).
- Tax revenues could be dramatically lower or higher than the $1.4 billion estimate; for example, uncertainty about the federal response to California legalization can swing estimates in either direction.
- Previous studies find that the annual cost of enforcing marijuana laws ranges from around $200 million to nearly $1.9 billion; our estimates show that the costs are probably less than $300 million.
- There is considerable uncertainty about the impact that legalizing marijuana in California would have on public budgets and consumption, with even minor changes in assumptions leading to major differences in outcomes.
- Much of the research used to inform this debate is based on insights from studies that examine small changes in marijuana prices or the risk of being sanctioned for possession. The proposed legislation in California would create a large change in policy. As a result, it is uncertain how useful these studies are for making projections about marijuana legalization.

Legalization has many potential dimensions; thus, the term can mean many different things (MacCoun and Reuter, 2001). An examination of the Dutch system, the Australian and Alaskan home-cultivation allowances, and the far more-extensive international experiences with alcohol and tobacco regulation suggests that the devil is in the details. On many dimensions, neither the Ammiano bill nor the RCTC proposition is particularly good at the details. Indeed, many of the issues addressed in this paper are specific to the "details" of these two proposals, not to marijuana legalization in general.

Limitations

This paper is not intended to be a complete evaluation of the consequences of the RCTC proposition or the Ammiano bill. A full cost-benefit analysis of marijuana legalization would include a number of items that have not been addressed here. For example, we have given no consideration to the reduction in government intrusiveness that comes from eliminating tens of thousands of marijuana arrests, many of which lead to criminal records for individuals who would otherwise have none. We have also not considered the effects that California legalization could have on gang activity in California or the drug-related violence in Mexico. Further, some would argue that a full analysis should also consider the benefits that users obtain from consuming marijuana and how this would change under a legalization regime. We do not ignore these factors because we think they are unimportant; rather, we thought it most constructive to focus on those areas in which we believe we can provide the most insight and that are novel or central to the debate about legalization in California in 2010, as opposed to the familiar general arguments concerning legalization in the abstract. We believe that the issues analyzed here are important for voters and legislators, perhaps particularly for those who are not already firmly in the pro- or antilegalization camps.

Finally, we stress that the marijuana situation in California is in great flux. No one should assume that the alternative to legalization is a static status quo. On one hand, the situation is getting tougher for users, as there has been a striking 30-percent increase in marijuana arrests in California since 2005. Further, the City of Los Angeles is now attempting to close more than 400 medical-marijuana dispensaries. On the other hand, there are indications that California could become more marijuana-friendly regardless of legalization. For example, medical-marijuana delivery services are proliferating (Cohn and Montgomery, 2010), at least one jurisdiction is talking about establishing industrial-scale growing operations for medical marijuana (Rayburn, 2010), and there are reports that growers are making marijuana more available and less expensive (Montgomery, 2010). Indeed, changes are occurring in California on several fronts, and it will likely be an altered state regardless of whether legalization passes.

Bibliography

ABC—*See* California Department of Alcoholic Beverage Control.

Abt Associates, *What America's Users Spend on Illegal Drugs 1988–2000*, Washington, D.C.: Executive Office of the President, Office of National Drug Control Policy, December 2001. As of June 28, 2010:
http://purl.access.gpo.gov/GPO/LPS20925

ADP—*See* California Department of Alcohol and Drug Programs.

Aegerter, Brenna, Karen M. Klonsky, and Richard L. De Moura, *Sample Costs to Establish and Produce Asparagus: San Joaquin Valley North, San Joaquin Valley*, Davis, Calif.: University of California Cooperative Extension, AS-VN-07, 2007. As of June 15, 2010:
http://coststudies.ucdavis.edu/files/asparagusvn2007.pdf

Alamar, Benjamin, Leila Mahmoud, and Stanton A. Glantz, *Cigarette Smuggling in California: Fact and Fiction*, San Francisco, Calif.: University of California, San Francisco, Center for Tobacco Control Research and Education, July 2003. As of June 28, 2010:
http://repositories.cdlib.org/ctcre/tcpmus/Smuggling2003

Albert-Goldberg, Nancy, "Los Angeles County Public Defender Office in Perspective," *California Western Law Review*, Vol. 45, No. 2, Spring 2009, pp. 445–474.

Amsterdam Tourist Information, "In 2010, Will There Be No More Coffeeshops in the Netherlands?" *DutchAmsterdam.nl*, November 19, 2008. As of June 28, 2010:
http://www.dutchamsterdam.nl/545-coffeeshops-netherlands

Anderson, Todd, Anna Cook, and Judith L. Wagner, *Medicaid's Reimbursements to Pharmacies for Prescription Drugs*, Washington, D.C.: Congressional Budget Office, 2004. As of June 28, 2010:
http://www.cbo.gov/ftpdocs/60xx/doc6038/12-16-Medicaid.pdf

Aos, Steven, Marna Geyer Miller, and Elizabeth Drake, *Evidence-Based Public Policy Options to Reduce Future Prison Construction, Criminal Justice Costs, and Crime Rates*, Olympia, Wash.: Washington State Institute for Public Policy, 06-10-1201, October 2006. As of June 30, 2010:
http://www.wsipp.wa.gov/pub.asp?docid=06-10-1201

Aos, Steven, Polly Phipps, Robert Barnoski, and Roxanne Lieb, *The Comparative Costs and Benefits of Programs to Reduce Crime: A Review of National Research Findings with Implications for Washington State*, version 4.0, Olympia, Wash.: Washington State Institute for Public Policy, 01-05-1201, May 2001. As of June 30, 2010:
http://www.wsipp.wa.gov/rptfiles/costbenefit.pdf

Askari, Hossein, and John Thomas Cummings, "Estimating Agricultural Supply Response with the Nurlove Model: A Survey," *International Economic Review*, Vol. 18, No. 2, June 1977, pp. 257–292.

Birnbaum, Howard G., Alan G. White, Jennifer L. Reynolds, Paul E. Greenberg, Mingliang Zhang, Sue Vallow, Jeff R. Schein, and Nathaniel P. Katz, "Estimated Costs of Prescription Opioid Analgesic Abuse in the United States in 2001: A Societal Perspective," *Clinical Journal of Pain*, Vol. 22, No. 8, October 2006, pp. 667–676.

Blank, Steve, Agricultural and Resource Economics Department, University of California, Davis, "Farm Household Profit Performance," undated briefing. As of June 4, 2010:
http://www.agecon.ucdavis.edu/extension/presentations/files/blank/farm_household_profit_performance.pdf

Blows, Stephanie, Rebecca Q. Ivers, Jennie Connor, Shanthi Ameratunga, Mark Woodward, and Robyn Norton, "Marijuana Use and Car Crash Injury," *Addiction*, Vol. 100, No. 5, May 2005, pp. 605–611.

BOE—*See* California Board of Equalization.

Bond, Brittany M., and Jonathan P. Caulkins, *Potential for Legal Marijuana Sales in California to Supply Rest of U.S.*, Santa Monica, Calif.: RAND Corporation, WR-765, 2010. As of June 30, 2010:
http://www.rand.org/pubs/working_papers/WR765/

Bonnie, Richard J., and Charles H. Whitebread II, "The Forbidden Fruit and the Tree of Knowledge: An Inquiry into the Legal History of American Marijuana Prohibition," *Virginia Law Review*, Vol. 56, No. 6, October 1970, pp. 971–1203.

Bouchard, Martin, "Towards a Realistic Method to Estimate the Cannabis Production in Industrialized Countries," *Contemporary Drug Problems*, Vol. 35, July 1, 2008, pp. 291–300.

Bramness, Jørgen G., Hassan Zaré Khiabani, and Jörg Mørland, "Impairment Due to Cannabis and Ethanol: Clinical Signs and Additive Effects," *Addiction*, Vol. 105, No. 6, June 2010, pp. 1080–1087.

California Assembly Bill 2254, February 18, 2010.

California Board of Equalization, *Preliminary Estimates of California Cigarette Tax Evasion*, June 1999.

———, *Staff Legislative Bill Analysis: SB 602*, May 20, 2009a. As of June 28, 2010:
http://www.boe.ca.gov/legdiv/pdf/sb0602-2jc.pdf

———, *Staff Legislative Bill Analysis: AB 390*, July 15, 2009b. As of June 28, 2010:
http://www.boe.ca.gov/legdiv/pdf/ab0390-1dw.pdf

California Department of Alcohol and Drug Programs, *Highlights of the Governor's Budget Fiscal Year 2010–11*, January 8, 2010. As of June 30, 2010:
http://www.adp.ca.gov/Admin/pdf/FY_2010-11_Governor%27s_Budget_Highlights.pdf

California Department of Alcoholic Beverage Control, "Alcoholic Beverage Licenses as of June 30, 2009," ABC-536, July 2009. As of June 30, 2010:
http://www.abc.ca.gov/datport/SubAnnStatRep.pdf

California Department of Corrections and Rehabilitation, *California Prisoners and Parolees (Annual)*, Sacramento, Calif., 2008a.

———, *Fourth Quarter Facts and Figures*, Sacramento, Calif., 2008b.

California Department of Public Health, "Medical Marijuana Program (MMP) Facts and Figures," June 9, 2010. As of June 28, 2010:
http://www.cdph.ca.gov/programs/MMP/Documents/Web%20Fact%20Sheet%206-9-10.pdf

California Department of Transportation, *Federal Highway Administration Amended Disadvantaged Business Enterprise Goal and Methodology: Federal Fiscal Year 2009*, undated. As of June 28, 2010:
http://www.dot.ca.gov/hq/bep/documents/GandMAmended.pdf

California National Organization for the Reform of Marijuana Laws, "Medical Marijuana Collectives Index: California Dispensary Locator," undated web page. As of June 28, 2010:
http://canorml.org/prop/cbclist.html

California NORML—*See* California National Organization for the Reform of Marijuana Laws.

California Senate Bill 1449, amended April 5, 2010.

Cameron, Lisa Ann, and Jenny Williams, "Substitutes or Complements? Alcohol, Cannabis, and Tobacco," *Economic Record*, Vol. 77, 2001, pp. 19–34.

Canadian Centre for Occupational Health and Safety, "Substance Abuse in the Workplace," modified June 15, 2008. As of June 3, 2010:
http://www.ccohs.ca/oshanswers/psychosocial/substance.html

Canelon, Raiza, "Los Olivos Town Hall to Focus on Medical-Marijuana Dispensary," *Santa Maria Times*, November 29, 2009. As of June 28, 2010:
http://www.santamariatimes.com/news/local/govt-and-politics/article_679b562a-dd78-11de-b964-001cc4c002e0.html

Caulkins, Jonathan P., *Cost of Marijuana Prohibition on the California Criminal Justice System*, Santa Monica, Calif.: RAND Corporation, WR-763, 2010a. As of June 30, 2010:
http://www.rand.org/pubs/working_papers/WR763/

———, *Estimated Cost of Production for Legalized Cannabis*, Santa Monica, Calif.: RAND Corporation, WR-764, 2010b. As of June 30, 2010:
http://www.rand.org/pubs/working_papers/WR764

Caulkins, Jonathan P., Eric Morris, and Rhajiv Ratnatunga, *Smuggling and Excise Tax Evasion for Legalized Marijuana*, Santa Monica, Calif.: RAND Corporation, WR-766, 2010. As of June 30, 2010:
http://www.rand.org/pubs/working_papers/WR766/

Caulkins, Jonathan P., and Rosalie Liccardo Pacula, "Marijuana Markets: Inferences from Reports by the Household Population," *Journal of Drug Issues*, Vol. 36, No. 1, Winter 2006, pp. 173–200.

Caulkins, Jonathan P., Rosalie Liccardo Pacula, Susan M. Paddock, and James Chiesa, *School-Based Drug Prevention: What Kind of Drug Use Does It Prevent?* Santa Monica, Calif.: RAND Corporation, MR-1459-RWJ, 2002. As of June 28, 2010:
http://www.rand.org/pubs/monograph_reports/MR1459/

Caulkins, Jonathan P., and Rema Padman, "Quantity Discounts and Quality Premia for Illicit Drugs," *Journal of the American Statistical Association*, Vol. 88, No. 423, September 1993, pp. 748–757.

Caulkins, Jonathan P., and Peter Reuter, "What Can We Learn from Drug Prices?" *Journal of Drug Issues*, Vol. 28, No. 3, 1998, pp. 593–612.

———, "How Drug Enforcement Affects Drug Prices," *Crime and Justice: A Review of Research*, Vol. 39, Fall 2010.

Caulkins, Jonathan P., C. Peter Rydell, William Schwabe, and James Chiesa, *Mandatory Minimum Drug Sentences: Throwing Away the Key or the Taxpayers' Money?* Santa Monica, Calif.: RAND Corporation, MR-827-DPRC, 1997. As of June 30, 2010:
http://www.rand.org/pubs/monograph_reports/MR827/

Cervantes, Jorge, *Marijuana Horticulture: The Indoor/Outdoor Medical Grower's Bible*, Sacramento, Calif.: Van Patten Publishing, 2006.

Chaloupka, Frank J., and Michael Grossman, *Price, Tobacco Control Policies and Youth Smoking*, Cambridge, Mass.: National Bureau of Economic Research, working paper 5740, September 1996. As of June 28, 2010:
http://www.nber.org/papers/w5740

Chaloupka, Frank J., Michael Grossman, and John A. Tauras, "The Demand for Cocaine and Marijuana by Youth," in Frank J. Chaloupka, Michael Grossman, W. K. Bickel, and H. Saffer, eds., *The Economic Analysis of Substance Use and Abuse: An Integration of Econometric and Behavioral Economic Research*, Chicago, Ill.: University of Chicago Press, 1999, pp. 133–156.

Chaloupka, Frank J., and Adit Laixuthai, "Do Youths Substitute Alcohol and Marijuana? Some Econometric Evidence," *Eastern Economic Journal*, Vol. 23, No. 3, Summer 1997, pp. 253–276.

CJSC—*See* Criminal Justice Statistics Center, Office of the Attorney General, State of California.

Clements, Kenneth W., and Xueyan Zhao, *Economics and Marijuana: Consumption, Pricing and Legalisation*, Cambridge, UK: Cambridge University Press, 2009.

Cline, Mike, "Convenience Store," San Antonio, Texas: SBDCNet, September 7, 2004. As of June 28, 2010:
http://sbdcnet.org/Snaphots/convenienceStore.pdf

Cochran, Mark J., Tony E. Windham, and Billy Moore, *Feasibility of Industrial Hemp Production in Arkansas*, University of Arkansas, Department of Agricultural Economics and Agribusiness, Cooperative Extension Service, May 2000. As of June 15, 2010:
http://www.votehemp.com/PDF/Hemp-Feasability-UofA.pdf

Cohn, Gary, and Michael Montgomery, "Marijuana Delivery Services Evade Bans on Dispensaries, Spread Across California," *Southern California Public Radio*, June 5, 2010. As of June 28, 2010:
http://scpr.org/news/2010/06/05/marijuana-delivery-services-evade-bans-dispensarie/

Cooley, Steve, district attorney, Los Angeles County, "Re: Initiative Measure 09-0024," memorandum, April 19, 2010. As of June 28, 2010:
http://www.californiapolicechiefs.org/nav_files/marijuana_files/files/MarijuanaInitiativeMeasure09-0024.pdf

Coté, John, Erin Allday, Wyatt Buchanan, and Marisa Lagos, "Feds Say S.F. Has More Pot Clubs Than Starbucks, but It Might Not Add Up," *SFGate.com*, November 18, 2008. As of June 30, 2010:
http://articles.sfgate.com/2008-11-18/bay-area/17127968_1_dispensaries-pot-clubs-medical-marijuana

County of Los Angeles Breath, "California Pharmacy Facts," revised May 2006. As of June 27, 2010:
http://www.colab-ala.org/tools_pharm_facts.htm

Cozac, D., "Rulings in Argentinean and Colombian Courts Decriminalize Possession of Small Amounts of Narcotics," *HIV/AIDS Policy and Law Review*, Vol. 14, No. 2, December 2009, pp. 54–55.

Crancer, Alfred, and Alan Crancer, *The Involvement of Marijuana in California Fatal Motor Vehicle Crashes 1998–2008*, June 2010. As of June 30, 2010:
http://druggeddriving.org/pdfs/CAMJStudyJune2010.pdf

Criminal Justice Statistics Center, Office of the Attorney General, State of California, *Report on Drug Arrests in California from 1990 to 1999*, undated (a). As of June 29, 2010:
http://www.ag.ca.gov/cjsc/pubs.php#drugArrests

———, "Statistics by City and County: CJSC Tables," undated web page (b). As of June 29, 2010:
http://ag.ca.gov/cjsc/datatabs.php

Day, Kevin R., Karen M. Klonsky, and Richard L. De Moura, *Sample Costs to Establish and Produce Pomegranates: San Joaquin Valley South, Furrow Irrigation*, Davis, Calif.: University of California Cooperative Extension, PG-VS-10, 2010. As of June 28, 2010:
http://coststudies.ucdavis.edu/files/pomegranatevs2010.pdf

Dean Runyan Associates, *California Travel Impacts by County, 1992–2008: 2009 Preliminary State and Regional Estimates*, Sacramento, Calif.: California Travel and Tourism Commission, April 2010. As of June 28, 2010:
http://tourism.visitcalifornia.com/media/uploads/files/editor/Research/CA09pRptrev.pdf

DeSimone, Jeffrey, "Is Marijuana a Gateway Drug?" *Eastern Economic Journal*, Vol. 24, No. 1, Spring 1998, pp. 149–164.

DeSimone, Jeffrey, and Matthew C. Farrelly, "Price and Enforcement Effects on Cocaine and Marijuana Demand," *Economic Inquiry*, Vol. 41, No. 1, January 2003, pp. 98–115.

DOJ—*See* U.S. Department of Justice.

Drug Availability Steering Committee, *Drug Availability Estimates in the United States*, Washington, D.C.: Office of National Drug Control Policy, 2002. As of June 28, 2010:
http://purl.access.gpo.gov/GPO/LPS49658

Dussault, C., M. Brault, J. Bouchard, and A. M. Lemire, "The Contribution of Alcohol and Other Drugs Among Fatally Injured Drivers in Quebec: Some Preliminary Results," in D. R. Mayhew and C. Dussault, eds., *Alcohol, Drugs and Traffic Safety*, Quebec: Société de l'assurance automobile du Québec, August 2002, pp. 423–430.

E Source Companies, "Managing Energy Costs in Grocery Stores," *Commercial Energy Advisor*, 2006. As of June 28, 2010:
http://www.esource.com/BEA/demo/PDF/CEA_groceries.pdf

Edwards, Logan, *Grow Great Marijuana: An Uncomplicated Guide to Growing the World's Finest Cannabis*, Los Angeles, Calif.: Sweetleaf, 2006.

Ehrensing, D. T., *Feasibility of Industrial Hemp Production in the United States Pacific Northwest*, Corvallis, Ore.: Agricultural Experiment Station, Oregon State University, station bulletin 681, May 1998. As of June 28, 2010:
http://hdl.handle.net/1957/13306

Elitzak, Howard, "Food Industry Costs, Profits, and Productivity," *Food Cost Review, 1950–97*, Washington, D.C.: Economic Research Service, agricultural economic report AER780, June 1, 1999, pp. 12–19. As of June 28, 2010:
http://www.ers.usda.gov/publications/aer780/

EMCDDA—*See* European Monitoring Centre for Drugs and Drug Addiction.

European Monitoring Centre for Drugs and Drug Addiction, "Table TDI-3: New Clients Entering Treatment by Primary Drug, 1997 to 2007, Part IV: New Cannabis Clients by Country and Year of Treatment (%)," *Statistical Bulletin 2009: Treatment Demand Indicator (TDI)*, Lisbon, c. 2009. As of July 1, 2010:
http://www.emcdda.europa.eu/stats09/tditab3d

Fake, Cindy, Karen M. Klonsky, and Richard L. De Moura, *Sample Costs to Produce Mixed Vegetables— Tomatoes, Winter Squash, Melons: Sierra Nevada Foothills, Placer and Nevada Counties*, Davis, Calif.: University of California Cooperative Extension, VM-IR-09, 2009. As of June 28, 2010:
http://coststudies.ucdavis.edu/files/MixedVegIR09.pdf

Farrelly, Matthew C., Jeremy W. Bray, Gary A. Zarkin, and Brett W. Wendling, "The Joint Demand for Cigarettes and Marijuana: Evidence from the National Household Surveys on Drug Abuse," *Journal of Health Economics*, Vol. 20, No. 1, January 2001, pp. 51–68.

FBI—*See* Federal Bureau of Investigation.

Federal Bureau of Investigation, *Crime in the United States, 1990–2008*. Data for 1995–2008, as of June 28, 2010:
http://www.fbi.gov/ucr/ucr.htm

First Research, "Convenience Stores and Gas Stations," industry profile, last quarterly update October 3, 2005.

Food Marketing Institute, "Marketing Costs," Arlington, Va., August 2008. As of June 28, 2010:
http://www.fmi.org/docs/facts_figs/MarketingCosts.pdf

Fortenbery, T. Randall, and Michael Bennett, "Opportunities for Commercial Hemp Production," *Review of Agricultural Economics*, Vol. 26, No. 1, Spring 2004, pp. 97–117.

Fries, Arthur, Robert W. Anthony, Andrew Cseko Jr., Carl C. Gaither, and Eric Schulman, *The Price and Purity of Illicit Drugs: 1981–2007*, Alexandria, Va.: Institute for Defense Analyses, P-4369, October 2008. As of June 28, 2010:
http://www.whitehousedrugpolicy.gov/publications/price_purity/price_purity07.pdf

Gettman, Jon, "Lost Taxes and Other Costs of Marijuana Laws," *Bulletin of Cannabis Reform*, September 5, 2007. As of June 28, 2010:
http://www.drugscience.org/Archive/bcr4/
Lost%20Taxes%20and%20Other%20Costs%20of%20Marijuana%20Laws.pdf

Gieringer, Dale H., *Economics of Cannabis Legalization: Detailed Analysis of the Benefits of Ending Cannabis Prohibition*, Washington, D.C.: National Organization for the Reform of Marijuana Laws, June 1994. As of June 28, 2010:
http://norml.org/index.cfm?Group_ID=4421

———, *The Origins of Cannabis Prohibition in California*, June 2006. As of June 28, 2010:
http://www.canorml.org/background/caloriginsmjproh.pdf

———, "Benefits of Marijuana Legalization in California," updated October 2009. As of June 14, 2010:
http://canorml.org/background/CA_legalization2.html

———, personal correspondence with the authors, May 28, 2010.

Graper, David F., and Rhoda Burrows, "Growing Asparagus," *Extension Extra*, Vol. 6009, September 2001. As of June 15, 2010:
http://agbiopubs.sdstate.edu/articles/ExEx6009.pdf

Grossman, Michael, "Individual Behaviours and Substance Use: The Role of Price," in Michael Grossman and Bjorn Lindgren, eds., *Advances in Health Economics and Health Services Research*, Vol. 16: *Substance Use: Individual Behaviour, Social Interactions, Markets and Politics*, Emerald Publishing Group Limited, 2005, pp. 15–39.

Grossman, Michael, and Frank J. Chaloupka, "The Demand for Cocaine by Young Adults: A Rational Addiction Approach," *Journal of Health Economics*, Vol. 17, No. 4, August 1998, pp. 427–474.

Grotenhermen, Franjo, Gero Leson, Günter Berghaus, Olaf H. Drummer, Hans-Peter Krüger, Marie Longo, Herbert Moskowitz, Bud Perrine, Johannes G. Ramaekers, Alison Smiley, and Rob Tunbridge, "Developing Limits for Driving Under Cannabis," *Addiction*, Vol. 102, No. 12, December 2007, pp. 1910–1917.

Hall, Wayne, and Louisa Degenhardt, "Adverse Health Effects of Non-Medical Cannabis Use," *Lancet*, Vol. 374, No. 9698, October 17, 2009, pp. 1383–1391.

Hall, Wayne, and Rosalie Liccardo Pacula, *Cannabis Use and Dependence: Public Health and Public Policy*, Cambridge, UK: Cambridge University Press, 2003.

Harris, Jeffrey E., and Sandra W. Chan, "The Continuum-of-Addiction: Cigarette Smoking in Relation to Price Among Americans Aged 15–29," *Health Economics*, Vol. 8, No. 1, February 1999, pp. 81–86.

Harwood, Henrick J., *Updating Estimates of the Economic Costs of Alcohol Abuse in the United States: Estimates, Update Methods, and Data*, Bethesda, Md.: U.S. Department of Health and Human Services, Public Health Service, National Institutes of Health, National Institute on Alcohol Abuse and Alcoholism, December 2000. As of June 30, 2010:
http://pubs.niaaa.nih.gov/publications/economic-2000/index.htm

Henning, Katherine J., *Grocery/Convenience Store Start-Up Profile*, Springfield, Ill.: Illinois Department of Commerce and Community Affairs, January 1998. As of June 28, 2010:
http://www.commerce.state.il.us/NR/rdonlyres/8D0B90B6-C149-437C-9C16-131E0D62CB9E/0/GroceryConvenienceStore.pdf

Hertel, Thomas W., "Applied General Equilibrium Analysis of Agricultural and Resource Policies," in Bruce L. Gardner and Gordon C. Rausser, eds., *Handbook of Agricultural Economics*, Vol. 2A: *Agriculture and Its External Linkages*, Amsterdam: North-Holland, 2002, pp. 1371–1419.

HHS—*See* U.S. Department of Health and Human Services.

Hoeffel, John, "L.A. City Council OKs Cap on Medical Marijuana Dispensaries," *L.A. Now*, December 8, 2009a. As of June 30, 2010:
http://latimesblogs.latimes.com/lanow/2009/12/la-city-council-oks-cap-on-medical-marijuana-dispensaries.html

———, "L.A. Acts to Cap Medical Marijuana Dispensaries," *Los Angeles Times*, December 9, 2009b. As of June 30, 2010:
http://articles.latimes.com/2009/dec/09/local/la-me-medical-marijuana9-2009dec09

———, "Los Angeles City Council Approves Medical Marijuana Ordinance That Will Shut Down Hundreds of Dispensaries," *L.A. Now*, January 26, 2010. As of June 28, 2010:
http://latimesblogs.latimes.com/lanow/2010/01/los-angeles-medical-marijuana-ordinance-pot-dispensaries.html

Hoppe, Robert A., "Million-Dollar Farms Dominate Production of Some Commodities," *Amber Waves*, March 2009. As of June 28, 2010:
http://www.ers.usda.gov/AmberWaves/March09/Findings/MillionDollarFarms.htm

Hoppe, Robert A., Penni Korb, Erik J. O'Donoghue, and David E. Banker, *Structure and Finances of U.S. Farms: Family Farm Report, 2007 Edition*, Washington, D.C.: U.S. Department of Agriculture, Economic Research Service, economic information bulletin 24, June 2007. As of June 28, 2010:
http://www.ers.usda.gov/Publications/EIB24/

Hu, T. W., H. Y. Sung, and T. E. Keeler, "Reducing Cigarette Consumption in California: Tobacco Taxes vs an Anti-Smoking Media Campaign," *American Journal of Public Health*, Vol. 85, No. 9, September 1995, pp. 1218–1222.

Hughes, A., N. Sathe, and K. Spagnola, *State Estimates of Substance Use from the 2006–2007 National Surveys on Drug Use and Health*, Rockville, Md.: Substance Abuse and Mental Health Services Administration, Office of Applied Studies, NSDUH Series H-35, HHS publication SMA 09-4362, 2009. As of June 28, 2010: http://www.oas.samhsa.gov/2k7state/toc.cfm

Hughes, Caitlin, and Alex Stevens, *The Effects of Decriminalization of Drug Use in Portugal*, Beckley Foundation Drug Policy Programme, briefing paper 14, December 2007. As of June 30, 2010: http://www.idpc.net/php-bin/documents/BFDPP_BP_14_EffectsOfDecriminalisation_EN.pdf.pdf

Idov, Michael, "Start Your Own. . . ," *New York Magazine*, February 19, 2006. As of June 28, 2010: http://nymag.com/guides/changeyourlife/16046/

"Inverse Relationship Between Sales and Profit Mix Narrows Slightly," *Convenience Store News*, June 1, 2009.

InvestorWords.com, undated website. As of June 6, 2010: http://www.investorwords.com/

Jacobson, Mireille, "Baby Booms and Drug Busts: Trends in Youth Drug Use in the United States, 1975–2000," *Quarterly Journal of Economics*, Vol. 119, No. 4, November 2004, pp. 1481–1512.

Johnston, L. D., P. M. O'Malley, J. G. Bachman, and J. E. Schulenberg, *Monitoring the Future*, annual. As of June 30, 2010: http://www.monitoringthefuture.org

Jones, R. K., David Shinar, and J. Michael Walsh, *State of Knowledge of Drug-Impaired Driving*, Washington, D.C.: National Highway Traffic Safety Administration, DOT HS 809 642, September 2003.

Joossens, Luk, and Martin Raw, "How Can Cigarette Smuggling Be Reduced?" *British Medical Journal*, Vol. 321, October 14, 2000, pp. 947–950.

Kandel, Denise B., *Stages and Pathways of Drug Involvement: Examining the Gateway Hypothesis*, Cambridge, UK: Cambridge University Press, 2002.

Kaufman, Phil R., "Rural Poor Have Less Access to Supermarkets, Large Grocery Stores," *Rural Development Perspectives*, Vol. 13, No. 3, October 1998, pp. 19–26. As of June 28, 2010: http://www.ers.usda.gov/publications/rdp/rdp1098/rdp1098c.pdf

Kenkel, Donald S., Alan D. Mathios, and Rosalie Liccardo Pacula, "Economics of Youth Drug Use, Addiction and Gateway Effects," *Addiction*, Vol. 96, No. 1, January 2001, pp. 151–164.

Kilmer, Beau, "Do Cannabis Possession Laws Influence Cannabis Use?" in I. Spruit, ed., *Cannabis 2002 Report: Technical Report of the International Scientific Conference*, Brussels: Ministry of Public Health of Belgium, 2002, pp. 119–141.

Kilmer, Beau, and Rosalie Liccardo Pacula, *Estimating the Size of the Global Drug Market: A Demand-Side Approach—Report 2*, Santa Monica, Calif.: RAND Corporation, TR-711-EC, 2009. As of June 28, 2010: http://www.rand.org/pubs/technical_reports/TR711/

King, Robert P., Ephraim S. Leibtag, and Ajay S. Behl, *Supermarket Characteristics and Operating Costs in Low-Income Areas*, Washington, D.C.: U.S. Department of Agriculture, Economic Research Service, December 2004. As of June 28, 2010: http://purl.access.gpo.gov/GPO/LPS100466

Kleiman, Mark A. R., *Against Excess: Drug Policy for Results*, New York: Basic Books, 1992.

———, "Enforcement Swamping: A Positive-Feedback Mechanism in Rates of Illicit Activity," *Mathematical and Computer Modelling*, Vol. 17, No. 2, January 1993, pp. 67–75.

"Kroger Company," *Columbus Dispatch*, undated web page. As of June 4, 2010: http://markets.dispatch.com/columbusdispatch/quote/profile?Symbol=321:945916

L.A. CLEAR, *2nd Quarter 2007 Drug Price List*, Commerce, Calif., c. 2008. As of June 30, 2010: https://www.laclear.com/Secure/Publications/2nd%20Qtr%20Tri-fold%20drug%20price%20list.pdf

LaFaive, Michael D., Patrick Fleenor, and Todd Nesbit, *Cigarette Taxes and Smuggling: A Statistical Analysis and Historical Review*, Midland, Mich.: Mackinac Center for Public Policy, December 2, 2008. As of June 30, 2010:
http://www.mackinac.org/10005

Larson, Richard C., and Amedeo R. Odoni, *Urban Operations Research*, Englewood Cliffs, N.J.: Prentice-Hall, 1981.

Leggett, T., "A Review of the World Cannabis Situation," *Bulletin on Narcotics*, Vol. 58, No. 1–2, 2006, pp. 1–3. As of June 28, 2010:
http://www.unodc.org/documents/data-and-analysis/bulletin/2006/
A_review_of_the_world_cannabis_situation.pdf

Lewit, Eugene M., and Douglas Coate, *The Potential for Using Excise Taxes to Reduce Smoking*, Cambridge, Mass.: National Bureau of Economic Research, working paper W0764, 1981.

MacCoun, Robert J., "Drugs and the Law: A Psychological Analysis of Drug Prohibition," *Psychological Bulletin*, Vol. 113, No. 3, 1993, pp. 497–512. Reprint available, as of June 28, 2010:
http://www.rand.org/pubs/reprints/RP209/

———, "In What Sense (If Any) Is Marijuana a Gateway Drug?" *Drug Policy Analysis Bulletin*, Vol. 4, 1998, pp. 5–8.

———, "California Assembly Bill 390 and the Tax and Regulate Cannabis Ballot Initiative: What Would Happen If California Legalized Marijuana?" presentation at the fourth annual conference of the International Society of the Study of Drug Policy, Santa Monica, Calif., 2010a.

———, *Estimating the Non-Price Effects of Legalization on Cannabis Consumption*, Santa Monica, Calif.: RAND Corporation, WR-767, 2010b. As of June 30, 2010:
http://www.rand.org/pubs/working_papers/WR767/

———, *What Can We Learn from the Dutch Cannabis Coffeeshop Experience?* Santa Monica, Calif.: RAND Corporation, WR-768, 2010c. As of June 30, 2010:
http://www.rand.org/pubs/working_papers/WR768/

MacCoun, Robert, Rosalie Liccardo Pacula, Jamie Chriqui, Katherine Harris, and Peter Reuter, "Do Citizens Know Whether Their State Has Decriminalized Marijuana? Assessing the Perceptual Component of Deterrence Theory," *Review of Law and Economics*, Vol. 5, No. 1, 2009, pp. 347–371.

MacCoun, Robert J., and Peter Reuter, *Drug War Heresies: Learning from Other Vices, Times, and Places*, Cambridge, UK: Cambridge University Press, 2001.

Mayberry, Keith S., *Sample Cost to Establish and Produce Asparagus: Imperial County, 2000*, Davis, Calif.: University of California Cooperative Extension, August 2000. As of June 28, 2010:
http://coststudies.ucdavis.edu/files/asparagus.pdf

McNeill, J. R., "Kif in the Rif: A Historical and Ecological Perspective on Marijuana, Markets, and Manure in Northern Morocco," *Mountain Research and Development*, Vol. 12, No. 4, November 1992, pp. 389–392.

Mikos, Robert A., "On the Limits of Supremacy: Medical Marijuana and the States' Overlooked Power to Legalize Federal Crime," *Vanderbilt Law Review*, Vol. 62, 2009, p. 1421.

Miron, Jeffrey A., *The Budgetary Implications of Marijuana Prohibition*, Washington, D.C.: Marijuana Policy Project, June 2005. As of June 28, 2010:
http://www.prohibitioncosts.org/

———, *The Budgetary Implications of Drug Prohibition*, Cambridge, Mass.: Harvard University, Department of Economics, February 2010. As of June 28, 2010:
http://www.economics.harvard.edu/faculty/miron/files/budget%202010%20Final.pdf

Miyao, Gene, Karen M. Klonsky, and Pete Livingston, *Sample Costs to Produce Processing Tomatoes: Transplanted in the Sacramento Valley*, Davis, Calif.: University of California Cooperative Extension, TM-SV-08-1, 2008. As of June 28, 2010:
http://coststudies.ucdavis.edu/files/tomatoessv1_2008.pdf

Moeller, K., *An Analysis of Costs and Profits in Two Copenhagen Cannabis Markets*, paper presented at the fourth annual conference of the International Society for the Study of Drug Policy, 2010.

Molinar, Richard H., Michael Yang, Karen M. Klonsky, and Richard L. De Moura, *Sample Costs to Produce Cherry Tomatoes: San Joaquin Valley South, Small Farm*, Davis, Calif.: University of California Cooperative Extension, TM-VS-05, 2005. As of June 28, 2010:
http://coststudies.ucdavis.edu/files/tomatochsjv2004.pdf

Montgomery, Michael, "Plummeting Marijuana Prices Create a Panic in Calif.," *All Things Considered*, May 15, 2010. As of June 28, 2010:
http://www.npr.org/templates/story/story.php?storyId=126806429

Musto, David F., "The Marihuana Tax Act of 1937," *Archives of General Psychiatry*, Vol. 26, No. 2, 1972, pp. 101–108.

National Drug Intelligence Center, "Marijuana," *Wyoming Drug Threat Assessment*, December 2001. As of June 28, 2010:
http://www.justice.gov/ndic/pubs07/712/marijuan.htm

———, *National Drug Threat Assessment 2009*, Johnstown, Pa., 2008-Q0317-005, December 2008. As of June 28, 2010:
http://www.justice.gov/dea/concern/18862/ndic_2009.pdf

National Institute on Drug Abuse, *Potency Monitoring Project: Report 100—December 16, 2007 Thru March 15, 2008*, University, Miss., c. 2008. As of June 28, 2010:
http://www.whitehousedrugpolicy.gov/pdf/FullPotencyReports.pdf

National Organization for the Reform of Marijuana Laws, "State Hemp Laws," updated April 10, 2002. As of June 15, 2010:
http://norml.org/index.cfm?Group_ID=3395

NDIC—*See* National Drug Intelligence Center.

"Netherlands Court: Five Cannabis Plants Allowed at All Times," *NIS News Bulletin*, December 23, 2008. As of June 30, 2010:
http://www.nisnews.nl/public/201208_2.htm

NIDA—*See* National Institute on Drug Abuse.

Non-Smokers' Rights Association, "Contraband Tobacco," Toronto, Ont., Spring 2009. As of June 30, 2010:
http://www.nsra-adnf.ca/cms/file/pdf/Contraband_Spring2009.pdf

Noy v. State, 83 P.3d 538, Alaska App., August 29, 2003.

NSRA—*See* Non-Smokers' Rights Association.

O*NET OnLine, "Summary Report for: 11-9011.01—Nursery and Greenhouse Managers," updated 2008. As of February 9, 2010:
http://online.onetcenter.org/link/summary/11-9011.01

O'Connell, Neil V., Craig E. Kallsen, Karen M. Klonsky, and Richard L. De Moura, *Sample Costs to Establish an Orchard and Produce Lemons: San Joaquin Valley South, Low Volume Irrigation*, Davis, Calif.: University of California Cooperative Extension, LM-VS-10, 2010. As of June 28, 2010:
http://coststudies.ucdavis.edu/files/lemonvs10.pdf

Office of National Drug Control Policy, "Prescription Drug Abuse Prevention," undated web page. As of June 3, 2010:
http://www.whitehousedrugpolicy.gov/drugfact/prescr_drg_abuse.html

———, *The Price and Purity of Illicit Drugs: 1981 Through the Second Quarter of 2003*, Washington, D.C., November 2004a. As of June 28, 2010:
http://www.ncjrs.gov/ondcppubs/publications/pdf/price_purity.pdf

———, *Technical Report for the Price and Purity of Illicit Drugs: 1981 Through the Second Quarter of 2003*, Washington, D.C., November 2004b. As of June 28, 2010:
http://www.ncjrs.gov/ondcppubs/publications/pdf/price_purity_tech_rpt.pdf

————, *ADAM II 2008 Annual Report: Arrestee Drug Abuse Monitoring Program II*, Washington, D.C., April 2009. As of June 28, 2010:
http://www.whitehousedrugpolicy.gov/publications/pdf/adam2008.pdf

————, *National Drug Control Strategy 2010*, Washington, D.C., 2010. As of June 28, 2010:
http://www.whitehousedrugpolicy.gov/publications/policy/ndcs10/index.html

Ogden, David W., deputy attorney general, U.S. Department of Justice, "Investigations and Prosecutions in States Authorizing the Medical Use of Marijuana," memorandum for U.S. Attorneys, October 19, 2009. As of July 1, 2010:
http://www.justice.gov/opa/documents/medical-marijuana.pdf

Pacula, Rosalie Liccardo, "Does Increasing the Beer Tax Reduce Marijuana Consumption?" *Journal of Health Economics*, Vol. 17, 1998a, pp. 557–585.

————, *Adolescent Alcohol and Marijuana Consumption: Is There Really a Gateway Effect?* Cambridge, Mass.: National Bureau of Economic Research, working paper 6348, January 1998b. As of June 30, 2010:
http://www.nber.org/papers/w6348

————, *Examining the Impact of Marijuana Legalization on Harms Associated with Marijuana Use*, Santa Monica, Calif.: RAND Corporation, WR-769, 2010a. As of June 30, 2010:
http://www.rand.org/pubs/working_papers/WR769/

————, *Examining the Impact of Marijuana Legalization on Marijuana Consumption: Insights from the Economics Literature*, Santa Monica, Calif.: RAND Corporation, WR-770, 2010b. As of June 30, 2010:
http://www.rand.org/pubs/working_papers/WR770/

Pacula, Rosalie Liccardo, Jamie F. Chriqui, and Joanna King, *Marijuana Decriminalization: What Does It Mean in the United States?* Cambridge, Mass.: National Bureau of Economic Research, working paper W9690, May 2003.

Pacula, Rosalie Liccardo, Michael Grossman, Frank J. Chaloupka, Patrick M. O'Malley, Lloyd D. Johnston, and Matthew C. Farrelly, "Marijuana and Youth," in Jonathan Gruber, ed., *Risky Behavior Among Youth: An Economic Analysis*, Chicago, Ill.: University of Chicago Press, 2001, pp. 271–326.

Pacula, Rosalie L., Robert MacCoun, Peter Reuter, Jamie Chriqui, Beau Kilmer, Katherine Harris, Letizia Paoli, and Carsten Schäfer, "What Does It Mean to Decriminalize Marijuana? A Cross-National Empirical Examination," in Björn Lindgren and Michael Grossman, eds., *Advances in Health Economics and Health Services Research*, Vol. 16: *Substance Use: Individual Behaviour, Social Interactions, Markets and Politics*, Amsterdam: Elsevier Press, 2005, pp. 347–370.

People v. Kelly (Patrick K.), 2010 Cal. LEXIS 623, Cal., January 21, 2010.

Perrine, M. W., Raymond C. Peck, and James C. Fell, *Epidemiologic Perspectives on Drunk Driving*, Washington, D.C.: U.S. Department of Health and Human Services, Public Health Service, Office of the Surgeon General, 1989. As of June 28, 2010:
http://profiles.nlm.nih.gov/NN/B/C/X/Y/_/nnbcxy.pdf

Piehl, Anne Morrison, and Geoffrey Williams, "Institutional Requirements for Effective Imposition of Fines," paper presented at Boalt Hall Law School, University of California, Berkeley, January 15, 2010.

Public Law 59-384, Federal Food and Drugs Act of 1906, June 30, 1906.

Public Law 75-238, Marihuana Tax Act, August 2, 1937.

Public Law 98-363, Uniform Minimum Drinking Age Act of 1984, July 17, 1984.

Public Law 100-690, Anti-Drug Abuse Act of 1988, November 18, 1988.

Ramaekers, J. G., G. Berghaus, M. van Laar, and O. H. Drummer, "Dose Related Risk of Motor Vehicle Crashes After Cannabis Use," *Drug and Alcohol Dependence*, Vol. 73, 2004, pp. 109–119.

Ravin v. State, 537 P.2d 494, Alaska, May 28, 1975.

Rayburn, Kelly, "Oakland Could Sanction Commercial Pot Grows," *Oakland Tribune*, June 3, 2010. As of June 28, 2010:
http://www.insidebayarea.com/ci_15214128

Reuter, Peter, *Disorganized Crime: The Economics of the Visible Hand*, Cambridge, Mass.: MIT Press, 1983.

———, "The (Continued) Vitality of Mythical Numbers," *Public Interest*, Vol. 75, Spring 1984, pp. 135–147.

———, *Marijuana Legalization: What Can Be Learned from Other Countries?* Santa Monica, Calif.: RAND Corporation, WR-771, 2010. As of June 30, 2010:
http://www.rand.org/pubs/working_papers/WR771/

Reuter, Peter, and Jonathan P. Caulkins, "Illegal 'Lemons': Price Dispersion in Cocaine and Heroin Markets," *Bulletin on Narcotics*, Vol. 56, No. 1–2, 2004, pp. 141–165. As of June 28, 2010:
http://www.unodc.org/pdf/bulletin/bulletin_2004_01_01_1_Art6.pdf

Reuter, Peter, Paul Hirschfield, and Curt Davies, *Assessing the Crack-Down on Marijuana in Maryland*, New York: Drug Policy Alliance, May 16, 2001. As of July 1, 2010:
http://www.drugpolicy.org/docUploads/md_mj_crackdown.pdf

Reuter, Peter, and Mark A. R. Kleiman, "Risks and Prices: An Economic Analysis of Drug Enforcement," *Crime and Justice*, Vol. 7, 1986, pp. 289–340.

Rhodes, William, Patrick Johnston, Song Han, and Quentin McMullen, *Illicit Drugs: Price Elasticity of Demand and Supply*, Cambridge, Mass.: Abt Associates, 2000.

Risk Management Association, *Grocery Stores*, undated study pack.

Robison, Wade, Roger Boisjoly, David Hoeker, and Stefan Young, "Representation and Misrepresentation: Tufte and the Morton Thiokol Engineers on the Challenger," *Science and Engineering Ethics*, Vol. 8, No. 1, January 2002, pp. 59–81.

Room, Robin, Benedikt Fischer, Wayne Hall, Simon Lenton, and Peter Reuter, *Cannabis Policy: Moving Beyond Stalemate*, Oxford, UK: Oxford University Press, 2010.

Rosenbloom, Stephanie, "The New Touch-Face of Vending Machines," *New York Times*, May 25, 2010. As of June 28, 2010:
http://www.nytimes.com/2010/05/26/business/26vending.html

Rydell, C. Peter, and Susan S. Everingham, *Controlling Cocaine: Supply Versus Demand Programs*, Santa Monica, Calif.: RAND Corporation, MR-331-ONDCP/A/DPRC, 1994. As of June 28, 2010:
http://www.rand.org/pubs/monograph_reports/MR331/

Saffer, Henry, and Frank J. Chaloupka, *State Drug Control Spending and Illicit Drug Participation*, Cambridge, Mass.: National Bureau of Economic Research, working paper W7114, 1999.

SAMHSA—*See* Substance Abuse and Mental Health Services Administration.

Samuels, David, "Dr. Kush: How Medical Marijuana Is Transforming the Pot Industry," *New Yorker*, July 28, 2008. As of July 1, 2010:
http://www.newyorker.com/reporting/2008/07/28/080728fa_fact_samuels

"San Jose City Council Discusses Pot Dispensary Regulation," *KTVU.com*, June 7, 2010. As of June 28, 2010:
http://www.ktvu.com/news/23826009/detail.html

Schwencke, Ken, and John Hoeffel, "Map: Marijuana Dispensaries Told to Close," *Los Angeles Times*, May 5, 2010. As of June 28, 2010:
http://www.latimes.com/news/local/la-me-closing-dispensaries,0,5206493.htmlstory

Semuels, Alana, "Marijuana Growers Upend Hard-Luck California Town," *Los Angeles Times*, November 1, 2009. As of June 28, 2010:
http://articles.latimes.com/2009/nov/01/business/fi-dope-county1

Slack, Adrian, Des O'Dea, Ian Sheerin, Ganesh Nana, Jiani Wu, and David Norman, *New Zealand Drug Harm Index: Report to the New Zealand Police*, Wellington: Business and Economic Research Ltd., April 2008. As of June 28, 2010:
http://www.berl.co.nz/754a1.page

Starrs, Paul F., and Peter Goin, *Field Guide to California Agriculture*, Berkeley, Calif.: University of California Press, 2010.

"Statistics: Indicators," *Amber Waves*, December 2009. As of June 28, 2010:
http://www.ers.usda.gov/AmberWaves/December09/Indicators/Indicators.htm

Substance Abuse and Mental Health Services Administration, Office of Applied Studies, "Quick Statistics from the Drug and Alcohol Services Information System," undated website. As of June 28, 2010:
http://wwwdasis.samhsa.gov/webt/NewMapv1.htm

———, *2004 National Survey on Drug Use and Health*, September 8, 2005. As of July 1, 2010:
http://oas.samhsa.gov/nsduh/reports.htm#2k4

———, *2005 National Survey on Drug Use and Health*, September 2006. As of July 1, 2010:
http://oas.samhsa.gov/nsduh/reports.htm#2k5

———, *2006 National Survey on Drug Use and Health*, September 2007. As of July 1, 2010:
http://oas.samhsa.gov/nsduh/reports.htm#2k6

———, *Results from the 2008 National Survey on Drug Use and Health: National Findings*, Rockville, Md., 2009.

———, *State Level Data on Alcohol, Tobacco, and Illegal Drug Use*, Rockville, Md., annual.

Taylor, Mac, legislative analyst, and Michael C. Genest, director of finance, Legislative Analyst's Office, letter to Edmund G. Brown Jr., attorney general, Sacramento, Calif., September 9, 2009. As of June 28, 2010:
http://www.lao.ca.gov/ballot/2009/090512.pdf

Thies, C., and C. Register, "Decriminalization of Marijuana and the Demand for Alcohol, Marijuana and Cocaine," *Social Science Journal*, Vol. 30, 1993, pp. 385–399.

Toonen, Marcel, Simon Ribot, and Jac Thissen, "Yield of Illicit Indoor Cannabis Cultivation in the Netherlands," *Journal of Forensic Sciences*, Vol. 51, No. 5, September 2006, pp. 1050–1054.

"Total Apple Consumption Hits Record Levels in 2004," *Apple News*, Vol. 36, No. 4, November 2005, pp. 1, 4. As of June 28, 2010:
http://www.usapple.org/media/publications/applenews/2005/nov2005.pdf

Tourte, Laura, Richard F. Smith, Karen M. Klonsky, and Richard L. De Moura, *Sample Costs to Produce Organic Leaf Lettuce: Double-Cropped Central Coast Region, Santa Cruz and Monterey Counties*, Davis, Calif.: University of California Cooperative Extension, LT-CC-09-O, 2009. As of June 28, 2010:
http://coststudies.ucdavis.edu/files/lettuceleaforganiccc09.pdf

Trim Scene Solutions, undated home page. As of June 30, 2010:
http://www.trimscene.com

Tufte, Edward R., *Visual Explanations: Images and Quantities, Evidence and Narrative*, Cheshire, Conn.: Graphics Press, 1997.

Tyler, Tom R., and Yuen J. Huo, *Trust in the Law: Encouraging Public Cooperation with the Police and Courts*, New York: Russell Sage Foundation, 2002.

United Nations Office on Drugs and Crime, *2005 World Drug Report*, Vienna, 2005.

———, *Bulletin on Narcotics: Illicit Drug Markets*, Vienna, 2006.

———, *World Drug Report*, New York, 2009.

University of California, Davis, Agricultural and Resource Economics, "Current Cost and Return Studies," last updated April 29, 2010. As of February 21, 2010:
http://coststudies.ucdavis.edu/current.php

Urada, Darren, Angela Hawken, Bradley T. Conner, Elizabeth Evans, M. Douglas Anglin, Joy Yang, Cheryl Teruya, Diane Herbeck, Jia Fan, Beth Rutkowski, Rachel Gonzales, Richard Rawson, Christine Grella, Michael Prendergast, Yih-Ing Hser, Jeremy Hunter, and Annie Poe, *Evaluation of Proposition 36: The Substance Abuse and Crime Prevention Act of 2000—2008 Report*, Department of Alcohol and Drug Programs, California Health and Human Services Agency, 2008. As of July 1, 2010:
http://www.uclaisap.org/prop36/documents/2008%20Final%20Report.pdf

U.S. Census Bureau, *2007 County Business Patterns*, 2007. As of June 30, 2010:
http://censtats.census.gov/cgi-bin/cbpnaic/cbpdetl.pl

———, "Sector 44: EC0744I1: Retail Trade: Industry Series: Preliminary Summary Statistics for the United States: 2007," *2007 Economic Census*, September 29, 2009. As of June 28, 2010:
http://factfinder.census.gov/servlet/
IBQTable?_bm=y&-ds_name=EC0744I1&-ib_type=NAICS2007&-NAICS2007=4442

U.S. Code, Title 23, Highways, Chapter 1, Federal-Aid Highways, Section 158, National Minimum Drinking Age.

U.S. Department of Agriculture, Economic Research Service, "Food Marketing System in the U.S.: Price Spreads from Farm to Consumer," updated May 7, 2008. As of June 28, 2010:
http://www.ers.usda.gov/Briefing/FoodMarketingSystem/pricespreads.htm

———, *2007 Census of Agriculture*, updated December 2009. As of June 28, 2010:
http://www.agcensus.usda.gov/Publications/2007/Full_Report/index.asp

U.S. Department of Health and Human Services, *Report to the President: Prescription Drug Coverage, Spending, Utilization, and Prices*, Rockville, Md., April 2000. As of June 28, 2010:
http://aspe.hhs.gov/health/reports/drugstudy/index.htm

———, *Treatment Episode Data Set—Admissions (TEDS-A): Concatenated, 1992 to Present*, April 6, 2009. As of June 28, 2010:
http://www.icpsr.umich.edu/icpsrweb/SAMHDA/studies/25221/detail

U.S. Department of Justice, Bureau of Justice Statistics, *National Judicial Reporting Program*, Washington, D.C., 2004.

U.S. Department of Labor, Office of the Assistant Secretary for Policy, "Working Partners for an Alcohol- and Drug-Free Workplace," undated website. As of June 28, 2010:
http://www.dol.gov/workingpartners/welcome.html

U.S. Drug Enforcement Administration, *Cannabis Yields*, Washington, D.C., 1992.

———, *Illegal Drug Prices and Purity Report*, Washington, D.C., 2003.

U.S. Energy Information Administration, "Average Retail Price of Electricity to Ultimate Customers by End-Use Sector, by State," *Electric Power Monthly*, June 16, 2010. As of June 30, 2010:
http://www.eia.doe.gov/electricity/epm/table5_6_b.html

U.S. General Services Administration, "Privately Owned Vehicle (POV) Mileage Reimbursement Rates," last reviewed April 29, 2010. As of June 4, 2010:
http://www.gsa.gov/Portal/gsa/ep/contentView.do?contentId=9646&contentType=GSA_BASIC

U.S. Growers Tobacco Company, "Tobacco Owners Calculator," undated web page. As of February 2, 2010:
http://www.usgrowerstobacco.com/USGTCCalc.htm

"US Growers Tobacco Company Creates New Marketing Opportunity," *Kentucky Agricultural News*, January 15, 2010. As of June 28, 2010:
http://www.kyagr.com/pr/kanonline/January152010/usgtc.htm

Uva, Wen-fei, and Steve Richards, *New York Greenhouse Business Summary and Financial Analysis, 2000*, Ithaca, N.Y.: Cornell University, College of Agriculture and Life Sciences, Department of Applied Economics and Management, EB 2002-03, February 2002. As of June 28, 2010:
http://hortmgt.aem.cornell.edu/pdf/resources/eb2002-03.pdf

Van Ours, Jan C., and Jenny Williams, "Cannabis Prices and Dynamics of Cannabis Use," *Journal of Health Economics*, Vol. 26, No. 3, May 2007, pp. 578–596.

Viscusi, W. Kip, and Joseph E. Aldy, "The Value of a Statistical Life: A Critical Review of Market Estimates Throughout the World," *Journal of Risk and Uncertainty*, Vol. 27, No. 1, August 2003, pp. 5–76.

Wheaton, James, attorney, "Initiative Measure 09-0024: 'Regulate, Control, Tax Cannabis,'" letter to Jerry Brown, attorney general of California, Sacramento, Calif., July 27, 2009. As of June 28, 2010:
http://ag.ca.gov/cms_attachments/initiatives/pdfs/i821_initiative_09-0024_amdt_1-s.pdf

"Wholesale Marijuana Prices," *Narcotic News*, undated web page. As of June 28, 2010:
http://www.narcoticnews.com/Marijuana-Prices-in-the-U.S.A.php

20.00

Wikinvest, "Whole Foods Market (WFMI)," undated web page. As of June 5, 2010:
http://www.wikinvest.com/stock/Whole_Foods_Market_%28WFMI%29

Williams, Jenny, "The Effects of Price and Policy on Marijuana Use: What Can Be Learned from the Australian Experience?" *Health Economics*, Vol. 13, No. 2, February 2004, pp. 123–137.

Williams, Jenny, and Parvin Mahmoudi, "Economic Relationship Between Alcohol and Cannabis Revisited," *Economic Record*, Vol. 80, No. 248, March 2004, pp. 36–48.

Williams, Jenny, Rosalie Liccardo Pacula, Frank J. Chaloupka, and Henry Wechsler, "Alcohol and Marijuana Use Among College Students: Economic Complements or Substitutes?" *Health Economics*, Vol. 13, No. 9, 2004, pp. 825–843.

———, "College Students' Use of Cocaine," *Substance Use and Misuse*, Vol. 41, No. 4, April 2006, pp. 489–509.

Wright, Doug, Joe Gfroerer, and Joan Epstein, "Ratio Estimation of Hardcore Drug Use," *Journal of Official Statistics*, Vol. 13, No. 4, 1997, pp. 401–416.

Zhao, Xueyan, and Mark N. Harris, "Demand for Marijuana, Alcohol and Tobacco: Participation, Levels of Consumption and Cross-Equation Correlations," *Economic Record*, Vol. 80, No. 251, December 2004, pp. 394–410.